Lesbians, Women and Society

First published in 1980, *Lesbians, Women and Society* presents an analysis of lesbianism as a phenomenon that developed from a 'personal problem' or 'individual deviance' to a social movement with political ambitions. Social lesbianism, an important concept introduced in the text, refers to the emergence of a public expression of lesbianism and is a stage in the process of establishing a lesbian group identity. It thrusts the issue into the public eye, and lends vitality to society's awareness. Two groups of 'social lesbians' are visible: those fearful of change who cling to traditional and social views, 'sick but not sorry'; and those who wish to challenge such traditional views in favour of a more public approach, 'sorry, but we're not sick.' But regardless of their relationships to the dominant sexual ideology, as a group, 'social lesbians' threaten the structure of power in society. This critical analysis thus challenges many people's views of lesbianism, and points out to the uninformed observer the complexities which are involved in the contemporary lesbian experience. This book will be of interest to students of sociology, gender studies, feminist theory, and sexuality studies.

I0084494

Lesbians, Women and Society

E. M. Ettorre

Routledge
Taylor & Francis Group

First published in 1980
by Routledge & Kegan Paul Ltd

This edition first published in 2022 by Routledge
4 Park Square, Milton Park, Abingdon, Oxon, OX14 4RN
and by Routledge
605 Third Avenue, New York, NY 10017

Routledge is an imprint of the Taylor & Francis Group, an informa business

© E. M. Ettorre 1980

Publisher's Note
The publisher has gone to great lengths to ensure the quality of this reprint but points out that some imperfections in the original copies may be apparent.

Disclaimer
The publisher has made every effort to trace copyright holders and welcomes correspondence from those they have been unable to contact.

A Library of Congress record exists under ISBN: 0710005466

ISBN: 978-1-032-33071-6 (hbk)
ISBN: 978-1-003-31813-2 (ebk)
ISBN: 978-1-032-33086-0 (pbk)

Book DOI 10.4324/9781003318132

Lesbians, Women and Society

E. M. Ettorre

Routledge & Kegan Paul
London, Boston and Henley

First published in 1980
by Routledge & Kegan Paul Ltd
39 Store Street, London WC1E 7DD,
Broadway House, Newtown Road,
Henley-on-Thames, Oxon RG9 1EN and
9 Park Street, Boston, Mass. 02108, USA
Set in IBM Press Roman 10/12pt by Columns
and printed in Great Britain by
Unwin Bros. Ltd.

British Library Cataloguing in Publication Data

Ettorre, E.M.

Lesbians, women and society.
1. Lesbianism
I. Title
301.41'57   HQ75.5   79-41237

ISBN 0 7100 0546 6
ISBN 0 7100 0330 7 Pbk

With love
To Isabel
Who teaches her friends integrity

Contents

Acknowledgments

The ideas in *Lesbians, Women and Society* were developed during the years from 1973-79. During that time many people gave me support and encouragement. I am grateful to all of them, especially my friends, many of whom are not mentioned here but who know who they are. Thanks.

In particular, I would like to thank: Terry Morris, my academic supervisor, for his unfailing confidence in my work; Margaret Jones for typing the original manuscript and, more importantly, for always listening; Jim Brown, for encouraging me initially to do this research; Jackie Foster from Sappho for helping me at various stages of my research; Keith Soothill for offering his 'publication suggestions' at my viva; Philippa Brewster from Routledge for her interest in my work as well as her helpful advice; all my former students who struggled with me and who helped me to be self-critical; Astra for her poem on celibacy and Carol Gardiner for her careful reading of the typescript. Thanks also to Tracey-Wren Setel for helping in revision of the Afterword.

There are others whose support and empathy were invaluable: Isabel, John, Luisa, Julia, Sandy, Margaret and Tim. I am grateful for their support and sharing their insights with me. I thank also my family, Ilona, Jim and Barbara from whom I learned that the experience of oppression and political struggle have the potential to create not only human consciousness but also the practice of equal, caring relationships, an implicit theme of this book.

For giving their time and for sharing their thoughts I have to thank all the lesbians who agreed to be interviewed as well as those women who were in any way involved in this research. I hope we will all become proud of our history, accept the struggles of the past, and progress to an awareness of our human potential. If lesbianism says anything in contemporary society, it says 'no' to the misuse of power. *Lesbians, Women and Society* makes this statement. Although there is one author, many are responsible for helping to make this statement.

E.M.E.

Introduction – Lesbianism:
a personal problem
or a women's issue

The subject of this book was originally the focus of my Ph.D. thesis in Sociology. I developed an interest in looking at homosexuality with a view to understanding its social implications for women. This book is about practice. It provides the reader with a brief insight into how lesbians live. But, more importantly, it tells us why lesbians, as a unique group of women, exist.

I wrote this book for 'real' people or for those who are more interested and concerned with creating a social understanding of feminism than with forming an intellectual élite.

During the course of my research, I met someone who said to me, 'It would be a good thing to have a book available that I could give to my parents and which would supply them with the answer to their questions about lesbianism.' Well, for you the reader, this book does not pretend to supply all the answers to the lesbian position in society. However, I hope it presents a comprehensible explanation which those who are interested and who meet up with some of these issues in the course of their work or lives may consciously apply.

This book is not free from drawbacks and has many limitations. First of all, this study is primarily a London-based study and therefore limited in geographical scope.

Second, although I was able to talk with at least 500 social lesbians over a period of four years, I was unable to reach those lesbians who were totally closeted or isolated. This obviously was an overwhelming limitation.

Third, from the point of view of mainstream feminist theory, or should I say what appears to be mainstream feminist theory, *Lesbians, Women and Society* does not address in any great detail those issues which have been labelled as substantive to the understanding of women's position in advanced capitalist society (i.e. the domestic labour issue, women as a reserve army of labour, female wage labour, the sexual

1

division of labour in the family, psychoanalysis and women and so on). This is because I attempt to deal with the issues directly and not to create a maze of jargon. This is not to imply that I feel that the above current feminist issues are not important. On the contrary, they remain important and interesting for a theoretical understanding of women's position. However, because this book is primarily concerned with practice I will deal with feminist issues which are relevant through practice. In other more academic contexts, I have and will deal with other theoretical issues. The stance for this book therefore necessitates having one's feet on the ground. It is not necessary for the reader to have an account of lesbianism via a circuitous route or from an obscure theoretical position.

Fourth, a major drawback of my thesis is the lack of any definite analysis of lesbianism and its relationship to social class. As of yet there has not been any development along these lines. This study has a middle-class bias. As you will discover, most of the lesbians in the study were middle-class. I do not mean to imply that there are no working-class lesbians. On the contrary, working-class lesbians do exist and form groups around their class as well as lesbian consciousness. However, this study concerns itself with that area of the lesbian ghetto which was accessible to those who could 'afford' to go to bars, clubs, meetings, and discos and who were able to spend their wages on the consumption of alcohol. In two particular cases I made an attempt to discuss my work with working-class lesbians. However, my attempts were thwarted, primarily because of the lack of interest in bourgeois sociology (and rightly so!)

Lesbianism and prior explanations of homosexuality

Previous explanations of homosexuality tended to individualize or personalize the experience. Furthermore, these studies were more concerned about homosexual men than lesbians. In light of these facts, there are two aims of this book. One is to make homosexuality relevant to society by showing its crucial social factors rather than any peripheral personal aspects. The second aim is to offset the existing male bias by emphasizing the effects of homosexuality on women. This book lays the foundation for a social theory of lesbianism. The theory is by no means conclusive and lends itself to further exploration.

Initially, certain issues should be clarified and will provide the foundation upon which an understanding of lesbianism will develop. The following questions are important: Why has there consistently been more concern for homosexual men than lesbians? How is homosexuality in general and lesbianism in particular analysed? What are the effects of these analyses? And how do previous analyses relate to the aims of this book?

Male domination and feminist practice

With the rise of women's consciousness, we are left with the ugly vision that society is male-dominated and that women have a secondary status. Feminist movements which challenge this form of dominance have continually emerged since the time when the suffragettes demanded votes for women.

In contemporary society, women's politics or feminist practice attempt to oppose social ideas about women – their 'female role', their reproductive function and their powerlessness as a social group. It should not be a revelation to us that women are usually viewed as underachievers and are also 'under-analysed' in most areas of social life, with the exception of the family, by the primary viewers (ideology makers). Women's problems, women's issues and women's ideas remain unnoticed or they appear as non-existent. Social theorists and those interested in explaining society, social change, social problems, etc. collude with society in making women invisible. Within the social problems area, the 'women's issue' is perceived more as a fact and less as a problem. This issue is irrelevant to the mainstream of social life. In relation to homosexuality, which, regretfully, has been analysed in the social problems area, women are also perceived in this way. Women in general and lesbians in particular are viewed as more sensitive, more vulnerable and more caring than men. They present less worry or need for social control.

If a woman is a lesbian, she is a potential mother. Most people believe that she, like all women, is *naturally* more caring than a homosexual man. In discussing this issue, one GP states:

It [lesbianism] is less of a problem; it is less evident; it was never subjected to such severe legal sanctions as those which were applied in the case of men. Being potential mothers, women are generally more caring except in the most severe pathological and sadistic cases.[1]

In light of the above, should we not consider that the reason for the seemingly unobtrusive or less threatening character of lesbianism relates directly to the general position of women in society? The 'domain of meaningful social action' has been reserved for men by men. Social scientists reflect this bias. On the theoretical level, concepts like women, feminine and female not only lack conceptual rigour but also suffer from, what I would term, analytical inferiority. This book upholds neither this inferiority nor male dominance. The emphasis on lesbianism rather than on homosexuality[2] in general or male homosexuality in particular is deliberate and, presumably, unnecessary, unimportant or 'deviationist' for some readers. However, many seemingly critical theories of homosexuality lack a feminist critique. I would contend that they remain partially correct, regardless of how substantive they appear to be. A theory that fails to advance an understanding of *all* forms of social dominance confuses the issue of women's oppression.

The social category 'homosexual' for either men or women may be viewed as an historical creation.[3] However, this should not lead us to assume and, furthermore, to analyse the experience of homosexual oppression as similar for both groups. A pivotal belief of this study is that patriarchy, male dominance and male power affect lesbians differently from gay men. (This will be discussed in more detail in Chapter 2, 'The social reality of lesbianism'.) Briefly, lesbianism exposes structural contradictions in or has negative effects on the structure of power[4] (which is society). The rise of feminist consciousness as well as gay consciousness for women has unique implications for lesbians in the struggle against male heterosexual oppression (sexual dominance). These new awarenesses may also help society to change this dominance. One lesbian viewed her new awareness in this way:

> 'My view of lesbianism has indeed changed. Well, I think at one time I regarded it as rather a bad thing, though if you had asked me for my views, I'd have defended it with my last breath. I used to feel that it was a bad thing to be a lesbian. But, now that society has changed so much, I don't feel that way any more. The whole awfulness of heterosexual relationships is coming up to the surface as well as women's place.'[5]

Hopefully, the findings of this study will offset this dominance and redress the balance. I have heard one person say, 'Dykes exist but even puffs have more power!' (The word, dyke, means lesbian, while puff refers to a gay man. If you are in doubt as to the meaning of any terms please refer to the Glossary of terms at the end of the book.)

Society's 'queer' model

Szasz[6] in his discussion of homosexuals as prime psychiatric scapegoats points out that their 'condition' and subsequent activity are considered as being morally wrong, medically diseased and psychologically disturbed (mentally sick). Homosexuality is viewed as deviant[7] or as a problem on the social level and as a sickness or a sin on the individual level. Homophobia,[8] society's fear of homosexuality, runs rampant and affects straights and gays alike. The latter group experience guilt, or are meant to experience it, for their deviance, while the former group oppose this threat to their acceptable social behaviour and remain fearful of its spread.

When homosexuality occurs it is consistently personalized, privatized and individualized in the attempt to stamp it out of existence. Doctors, psychiatrists, social workers, teachers and ultimately society itself tell homosexuals to hide their infirmity or social deformity.[9] As a result, individual homosexuals lose a sense of group awareness. They stop questioning why their oppression exists and negate their potential for social criticism. However, the struggle against this oppression does have other effects.

'I started out with society's definition of lesbianism. Then, if you think you are, you wonder how you fit into those expectations – those expectations of what society thinks a lesbian is. At the same time, you don't necessarily think of yourself as having a negative experience, although you know society thinks of your lesbianism as a negative experience. Also, inside, you feel a lot of guilt because you know that other people are going to be upset and that you might turn into another species for them. But, you're "doing for yourself" in a sense. Then gradually, you say something which is almost unconscious. When you speak it, it is definitely contrary to society's image of it. This is lesbian consciousness and it keeps on developing.'

'Lesbianism is a conscious knowledge. That is what lesbianism means to me as a women. It is definitely a feminist consciousness because

you see lesbianism in terms of feminism and you relate lesbianism to
yourself as a woman. You're not seeing lesbianism apart from the
fact that you are a woman. I mean you're not seeing it how society
sees it or you. Then it's not just another bit of you. Two things
are interconnected. You see your lesbianism with a feminist
consciousness. This means that you see your lesbianism in a
conscious way, not in a hidden or isolated way, rather than an
unconscious way or like those who lumber around a bar with it.'

Steps towards homosexual consciousness are subverted on both the
individual and social levels. The movement towards gay liberation is an
attempt to challenge this process. The slogan 'Glad to be Gay', which
emerged from the Gay Liberation Front in the 1960s was evidence of a
new trend towards group consciousness.[10] However, amidst the struggle
for gay liberation, lesbians oppressed within GLF discovered that the
above slogan really meant 'Glad to be Male and Gay'.[11] Lesbians also
became aware that the word 'homosexual' was just another 'male
concept' which reflected the interests of a dominant group.

'I must say that we're talking a lot these days about our gay
brothers. But, if you know anything about the gay movement in
England, you realize that gay men are in the same trip as straight
men. All gay men are interested in doing is getting *themselves*
organized. On [mentions a gay newspaper] , I think I'm right in
saying that they only have two women. They have token lesbian
articles . . . . As far as gay politics are concerned they ignore women.
I'm involved in lesbian politics. Women who get involved in gay
politics are, I feel, banging their heads against the wall. Gay men are
like straight men in that they couldn't give a fuck about women.'

Lesbianism: the 'unthinkable' reality

In the past, if someone was interested in the factors which explained
lesbianism, they looked for answers to questions such as Is a woman
born a lesbian? Do lesbians desire to be men? Was lesbianism just a
sexual preference, and Were lesbians sick, perverted or emotionally
imbalanced? Yet these questions may be attacked as irrelevant, as
forming an undercurrent of suspicion or as lacking an historical understanding. Regardless of these criticisms, we should be more concerned

with an historical approach.

The general public remains uninformed about lesbianism. Possibly, the typical social reaction – disgust – may inhibit any interest or concern. It is interesting to note, however, that lesbianism has a certain appeal in sex shops and in pornographic literature. Any form of disgust manages not only to keep well hidden but to be transformed into a source of titillation for the male fantasy. Yet on another level, the *real* existence of lesbianism is 'unthinkable'. Its existence is too threatening for society to give it serious thought. Abbott and Love say:

> If there are lesbians – women who fulfill one another sexually – then perhaps women are not the passive creatures men make them out to be. To recognize the existence of lesbianism is to admit that women are sexual beings in and of themselves and that they do not need, though they may want, men in this basic way. Such independence from men is a *de facto* challenge to the idea that women exist for men.[12]

Lesbians themselves say:

> 'Society doesn't realize it is there. It is more acceptable for two women to walk down the street holding each other than for two men to do the same. But anyways society looks on a woman as if she should be looking for a man. Lesbian couples are not ridiculed like gay men in couples. Straight women accept the lesbian set-up more than straight men. It's a real threat to men. They don't understand it.'

> 'We are female outcasts or outcast identities in society. I mean lesbianism is basically women with each other and this isn't given any credence in society. Because women aren't given a separate identity in society, women together aren't given any identity either. You don't count as a woman, if you are a lesbian.'

> 'If society is going to accept us, they have to accept us as we are, as lesbians – not that we are lesbians according to their conception which is really a male phallic conception of women. And if they do accept the whole of us as we are, then there is a lesbian identity and lesbians exist.'

Within their particular field, sociologists reflect dominant social opinions about lesbianism. In fact they avoid confronting it. Yet when they do analyse it, they view it as merely an adaptation to unnatural social settings (i.e. prison,[13] profession of stripping[14]). Very few[15] describe lesbianism as it relates to the general position of women in society.

To treat lesbianism as a type of feminist consciousness, as a threat to patriarchy and capitalism or as a struggle against the structure of power (power relations) has interesting implications. Labels such as 'absurd', 'meaningless', 'irrelevant', 'misplaced', 'ideological', 'deviationist', 'unimportant to the real issue', etc. may be tacked on to these feminist analyses. Critics may ask: 'How does lesbianism relate to the total structure of social relationships when sex is either a biological condition or a personal act within the total social labour process – labour done by all to keep society going?'

Ironically, those who criticize society's ability to dull revolutionary awareness do themselves possess this ability and do subvert consciousness. They appear to scrutinize with an 'air of political programming' all areas of social life. Barriers or divisions within society seem to break down. For these critics, the personal reflects the political; the private becomes public. Critical analysis is their key to opening the door of understanding and potential social change.

In reality, these critics divorce from their revolutionary scope and subsequent critical analysis those areas which appear as too threatening. They accuse society of splitting social reality or simply of creating unnecessary barriers and divisions. Yet, in a type of schizophrenic stupor, they do likewise.

In this way, sexuality is denied adequate social criticism. The assumption that sexuality and sexual relationships are unchanging, static or simply biological facts of life is made. These two categories are merely examined in relationship to the sexual division of labour which emerges from the family, i.e. man, husband produces and woman, wife, mother reproduces. There is little attempt to discuss sexuality outside the family context – the only valid area of analysis for 'true believers'[16].

The crucial issue of women's oppression slowly vanishes, while it becomes clear that these theorists have not learned their lesson from the past. Their sword of truth is blunted; the sanctity of the family is maintained. Women's position in society remains a cultural error, an historical, not hysterical, mishap. Therefore, it is dealt with on that level. Patriarchy, male dominance, male power, etc. equal CULTURE.[17]

In this context, lesbianism like all forms of sexual behaviour is relegated to a personal act. Like male homosexuality, it is a threat to the continuance of the family. Society is not comfortable with this presence, but it does not fully understand why this is so. How could society become fully aware if attempts at consciousness are being continually subverted?

It is a major contention of this book that lesbianism not only presents a challenge to the position of women in society but also questions the structure of power relations. If critically analysed, it exposes contradictions which exist between beliefs about biology and culture, the sexual and the ideological, women and femininity and production and reproduction. Lesbianism emerges from a dominant male heterosexual society, the basis for the cultural production of ideas.

Lesbianism should no longer be considered as an individual genetic quirk, a psychological malfunctioning, a mental illness, an immaturity, an abnormality or perversion. Causal explanations which lead to notions like 'arrested heterosexuality', 'dominant mother-figure', 'dominant father-figure', 'abnormal hormones' or 'faulty genetic composition' should be abolished. Explanations[18] of lesbianism should be rooted in history and based upon a social theory of sexuality. Correspondingly, a social theory of lesbianism should discuss the structure of society – patriarchy and capitalism – power relations *vis à vis* this structure, the social control of production and reproduction, the dominant groups such as heterosexuals and men who struggle to maintain this power, the social relations which result from this system of domination, the mechanisms by which this domination is ensured, and women's subordination within the social labour process.

In light of the above, this book does not pretend to be a far-reaching historical treatise on the subject. Nor does it pretend to be a definitive sociological study. It does, however, initiate two novel discussions. First, sexuality and related issues are discussed in new arenas outside the traditional family context. Second, lesbianism is thrust out into the open and emphasized more as a social phenomenon and less as a sexual preference or problem.

This book is feminist-based. It addresses itself not only to women's struggle against subordination but also to the *whole* question of subordination itself. The aim of this book is to challenge society's attitudes towards lesbianism and, therefore, to stir up future criticism in this area of debate.

I hope that in whatever perspective the reader finds her or himself (sociologist or not, political or not, feminist or not, socialist or not), she or he will come to a new awareness of lesbianism.

As implied earlier, this book is not meant to be a definitive social or psychological study. Rather, it is a descriptive and analytical account of the situation of lesbians in a large metropolitan area. However, this situation exposes the rise of what I term social lesbianism. I will argue that social lesbianism is rooted in an historical process. Lesbians are striving for something for themselves and for society. We may rightly ask 'What is this something?' Is it equality with men, equality with heterosexual women, freedom from homosexual oppression or an abolition of sex roles and the family? The answer to this crucial question will not be given completely in this text. The answer, however, will be approached with historical sensitivity.

The following chapter introduces a seed theory of lesbianism – its historical emergence and its development as social lesbianism. Chapter 2 describes the social reality of lesbianism and emphasizes important aspects of the lesbian identity as well as the variety of lesbian relationships which are possible. Chapter 3 examines the historical emergence of lesbianism and the implications of social lesbianism, while Chapter 4 offers a comparison of both groups. Chapter 5 discusses the potential for the formation of lesbian politics. Chapter 6 firmly places lesbianism within the context of a political struggle. The last chapter is an Afterword and presents a seed theory of lesbianism as it relates to other theories of power and sexuality.

Appendices are included and should prove useful in supplying the reader with facts about this study – how, when and where the research was carried out, and the characteristics of the lesbians involved. There is also a glossary of terms, which should enable the reader to have a quick grasp of important concepts.

The collection of lesbian data

During the beginning of my research I was able to meet with various lesbians and talk about their particular groups and the purposes of their organizations. Because I was a newcomer to the London lesbian scene, one woman who remained an important contact throughout the research volunteered to take me to a weekly meeting of a lesbian group and to introduce me to its organizer. My initiation into this lesbian group occurred in December 1974. This contact with a local lesbian group and its organizer proved to be important. It was at these weekly meetings that I soon became familiar with the London lesbian ghetto. I went along regularly to these meetings for a period of three years during the course of my research. It was through this particular lesbian organization 'Sappho', that I was able to distribute half of my questionnaires. I became known as a 'resident sociologist' and many women were willing to talk to me about my work.

The social context of the group was varied. However, one factor seemed to be consistent, namely, these weekly meetings afforded members a 'sociable' atmosphere in which lesbians could relax in the presence of other lesbians and within a bar context. Sometimes part of the meeting was taken up with speakers or discussion groups. However, socializing seemed to be the main function. Some lesbians told me that for a variety of reasons these gatherings were the only time when, in the course of a week, they could relax and be themselves in a totally lesbian context. The group varied in many ways. There were age differences from about 18-60 (average age about late 20s, early 30s). There was an ideological spectrum from lesbian activists, who tended to be in a minority, to non-political lesbians who tended to dominate the scene. There were various levels of outness from somewhat closeted lesbians to the open lesbians. The number of lesbian participants varied from about 30 to 60 members each week.

The wealth of information which I gathered at these weekly meetings was invaluable. I was able to establish relationships of trust with many of the lesbians with whom I came in contact. Gradually, most members came to know me as a sociologist and as a confidant with whom one could discuss one's life. In order to build up relationships of mutual trust and understanding, I would periodically distribute my written work. Usually, my work was read with enthusiasm and often I was provided with pages of criticism, which proved useful in sharpening my own analysis of the lesbian ghetto.

In January 1975, after attending Sappho for one year, my role of researcher was recognized by new members of the group, as well as accepted by regular members of the lesbian community.

Along with these regular meetings I went regularly to bars, clubs and discos which were either all-lesbian or mixed gay (gay men and lesbians). Also, I attended various women's groups. The women's groups usually had a lesbian caucus which formed a working section of the organization. The groups, organizations or conferences of which I was a member numbered about fourteen and my membership within these groups began in 1974.

Membership in these groups, conferences and organizations enabled me to come in contact with many different lesbians, all of whom had various levels of lesbian consciousness.

From June 1975 until June 1976 I collected the major bulk of my research data. Since I had already become a trusted member of the lesbian community, my contact with other lesbians expanded into social contexts outside of my initial weekly meetings. Frequently, I was invited to lunches, dinners, parties, social gatherings. Also during this time I went to gay bars, gay clubs, lesbian bars, lesbian clubs, discos, etc. regularly. My amount of contact with the lesbian ghetto grew as my research progressed. A 'promotion process' through the lesbian ghetto gave me acceptability in the ghetto, as well as validity in terms of my research role. It seemed to me that my analysis was becoming clearer and crystallized on a conceptual level.

At this particular time, I wanted to test out my research concepts and in early 1976 I distributed 700 questionnaires. In February 1976 I attended a national Lesbian Conference which I had assumed would be attended predominantly by political lesbians. I distributed 400 questionnaires at this time; 101 were returned to me by post. A month later (March) I distributed 300 questionnaires to lesbian magazine subscribers who were affiliated either directly (actually attended some of the meetings) or marginally (knew about the meetings) with my Tuesday evening group which had the same name as the lesbian magazine; 100 were returned to me.

In early February 1977, a year later, I was able to analyse my research findings from the questionnaires. It was at that time that I constructed a computer programme, Lestudy, in order to facilitate this analysis.

In March 1976 I began to conduct a series of interviews from which I collected valuable qualitative data which speaks for itself throughout the book. Interviews were carried out from March 1976 until December 1976. The lesbians I spoke with and interviewed were involved in all sorts of social activity, ranged in ages from 18 to 54 and differed in their ideas about lesbianism. I viewed the research task as a collective task in which I was able to establish a position on lesbianism only in and through the lesbian community and with the help of lesbians and others whom I met. Often my interviews became a collective task because I realized that many lesbians had much to contribute to a sociological understanding of lesbianism.

Interviews usually took place in people's homes, my flat, place of employment, or at college. They lasted from between 30 minutes to two and a half hours. The average time was 45 minutes. I preceded my taped interviews with a discussion of what I was doing, the guaranteed confidence of the information and a general rundown of why I thought it was important for a sociological discussion of lesbianism to be developed. My formal interviews (20) were taped and followed a definite interview schedule. However, I often asked other lead questions which followed along with the main questions of the interview. My untaped[19] interviews (40) usually centred around one or two lead questions, i.e., What is lesbianism? Why do you think you are a lesbian?

A final introductory note: the research imperative

There was a continual tension which was present for me during the entire research process. It was inescapable. Basically, the tension existed between the social scientific notion of 'objectivity' which demands detachment, distance and removal from what I was studying in order to be value-free, and the subjective experience of being a woman and a lesbian, which I am. It is important, therefore, that the reader is presented with the facts as they have existed. Before you delve into the major bulk of the research, you are aware of the researcher as both insider and outsider in the lesbian experience.

However, the following is a critical analysis of lesbianism. The observations, findings, data, etc. are presented as not only a detailed descriptive account but also an objective study. They are related to you as accurately as possible – as I have observed and recorded them, as other lesbians have observed and as other lesbians have related their experiences to me. Regardless of your attitudes towards the researcher's bias (that is seeing me more as a woman than as a lesbian sociologist, a sociologist of lesbianism or however you view me), you will be given the facts.

Initially, I became aware of my own biases, established them and looked beyond them for the facts. This process implied that I had an empathy with the subject area and recorded what I had observed whether or not I liked, agreed with or, furthermore, believed in what I had observed or been told. I established this as an operating principle in the study. This principle became my own personal imperative as an aware researcher.

The position put forward in *Lesbians, Women and Society* is feminist.

Therefore it is not separatist. This position calls for solidarity as well as the raising of consciousness on all levels for both women and men. It is a book about power and not about its misuse or an élitist appropriation of it.

I hope that the value of this book lies in the fact that its perspective illuminates in a new light the very world in which we all have lived our lives. Obviously, these lives involve varying degrees of struggle.

1 Sappho revisited: a new look at lesbianism

'Society doesn't like to give us any space to be ourselves openly, because we are an alternative. We're an alternative to heterosexuality, which is projected as the norm. We question just by being here, many values which are part of heterosexuality. We question women's dependence on men. We question male/female role-playing. We question the sexuality of every human being who thinks they're normal.

'What's so normal, natural, fulfilling about heterosexuality? Natural is what feels good, normal is feeling ordinary, fulfilled is when you just did what you felt like doing. Anyone can be any or all of these things and no one except themselves can possibly know whether or not they are. What is it that makes heterosexuals feel so insecure about themselves that they can allow no alternative sexuality? How solid are the foundations upon which they build their moral values?'[1]

In order to understand lesbianism, we should look at how it fits into both the culture and structure of society. (By 'culture', I mean the way of life of a particular society. By 'structure', I mean those social forces which determine that way of life.) We should view it as a complex social issue. In relationship to these two aspects of society, lesbianism poses a threat. As stated earlier, lesbianism exposes contradictions which exist in our beliefs about biology and culture, sex and ideology and women and femininity. By its very presence in society, it sheds light on such questions as: Does the source of the vast differences between men and women lie in biology or culture? Is the category 'sexual' only related to biology or is it related to culture and further- more, structure? How are biology and culture defined in society? Are women 'naturally female' and men 'naturally male' *or* does culture play a large part in defining femininity and masculinity? What is 'natural' or

15

'human nature'? Do they really exist *or* are our beliefs about sexuality based on a false foundation? And what are our ideas about sex really based on?

Whatever the answers to these questions may be, the fact still remains that lesbianism exists in a society which is heterosexual and male-orientated and whose culture produces sexual ideas with those dominant interests in mind.

Culture and sexuality

Sexual ideas develop in the light of specific biological bases (the sex organs). Yet these sexual ideas are also formed within and by concrete human experiences. Sex is viewed as a basic, material[2] need which must be satisfied. (Freud was keen on furthering this view and he predicted that individuals would have problems if their sex drive was left unfulfilled.) Furthermore, norms, the unwritten rules which govern behaviour, tell us that this 'powerful instinct' should be satisfied not only socially,[3] that is, with others – preferably, one other person of the opposite sex, but also according to certain characteristics – age, sex, race, class. Normal sexual performance or sexual behaviour which obeys sexual norms usually becomes a way of achieving a certain amount of social status.[4] When a dominant sexual viewpoint or sexual ideology is produced, it tends to be dependent upon how society processes and structures social relationships. In addition, this process appears directly related to *power*.

Many people experience culture as a way of life. However, it may also be experienced as a productive process which provides us with the tools to master the world about us. In the area of the 'sexual', culture further provides us with an unquestioning acceptance of a sexual instinct. Through socialization, culture presents vivid images and ideas of acceptable sexual behaviour. Through culture, sex becomes institutionalized or ritualized and ultimately imprints upon our minds a dominant sexual ideology. However, it is important to be aware that acceptable ways of satisfying a supposed basic material need are based upon one's biology and, moreover, culture's definition of this biology! Sex is structured or organized according to two sub-groupings, seen as 'naturally' distinct from one another – men and women. These two groups are physically different from one another and develop socially on the basis of the biological differences between each other. Yet, the entire physical or material world of which human sexuality is only a small part becomes clouded by these differences. A fundamental biological tension exposes itself and culture thrives on it. Possibly Freud was correct in suggesting that biology is destiny.

Culture perpetuates the idea that sex is a powerful drive as well as a physical need. Therefore, individuals should experience 'sex' not only as an uncontrollable desire but also as a basic impulse. As a result, sex is transformed from a physical base to human want or from material reality to a type of awareness. None the less, sexual activity remains a biologically discriminating process based on those who reproduce, women, and those who do not reproduce, men.

Power and sexuality

Earlier, I indicated that sexual relationships have to do with power. I would argue further that *all* social relationships are power relationships. These power relationships are established between people in the process of making society, which is a complex web of social relationships. This 'society' is capitalist – where people make money – and patriarchal – where women are subordinate to men in order for people to make sex and ultimately reproduce society. In other words, contemporary society has developed as a patriarchal capitalist society in which power lies in the hands of men and capitalists. Both of these groups reflect the results of how power is established, organized, distributed, mobilized and perpetuated in relationships between people in society. Both capitalism and patriarchy compose society's structure and reflect how people so far have made society. Thus, the most fundamental way of making society is through power relationships – male-directed or money-related or both. Hierarchy becomes the order of the day.

Within the above social organization of power, women lose out. They have less power and social value. Society places higher premiums on men, male activities, production in the factories and waged labour than on women, female activities, reproduction in the home and domestic or wageless labour.[5] Women are viewed in the truest sense of the word as the 'weakest' sex. They have little value as workers, as producers or as *real* money-makers. Women are members of a secondary workforce; men are members of *the primary* workforce. All of these ideas are embedded within our value system and become part of the dominant sexual ideology. Social value which is sex-based is measured by one's productive value (making money) rather than one's reproductive value (making babies). More simply, social status which is directly related to social value is grounded in productive labour (men's work) and *not* in child or reproductive labour (women's work). Ironically, however, women are absolutely essential for the continuation of any given society. As a social group, they are the *real* producers in society: the bearers of future generations. Why then does society deny women the social importance that is due to them? Perhaps, the answer lies within our understanding of women's biological vulnerability or periodical physical weakness, which, in our society, imply the need for protection. Regardless of our conceptions, is this 'weakness' in reality a strength? Observing this perplexing situation, Simone de Beauvoir states: 'The body of woman is one of the essential elements in her situation in the world. But, that body is not enough to define her as woman.'[6]

A woman, like a man, is her body. Yet, historically, she has been enslaved to it. Her reproductive function, which I term her 'species-producing power', has resulted in a limitation of her social power and a denial of her social value.

During the course of history, the forces of production – both the instruments and human labour through which material goods are produced – were and are generated under different economic conditions (factors which determined how people produced goods in the range of societies whether primitive, ancient, feudal or capitalist). A particular society not only governs how people in general relate but also determines sexual relations between men and women. This is how history has developed and how the forces of production have operated. However, within this view an important element is missing – the forces of reproduction. Where does one locate women's species-producing power? Throughout history, these forces have been constant and women have remained subordinate. In this way, the category 'sex' has emerged only to divide the development of our material world and to split human history!

Social thinkers speak of a 'sexual division of labour'. They describe this division as part of the social labour processes in which men are engaged in 'male' jobs and women function in 'female' tasks. This 'sexual division of labour' solidifies in the modern family structure. Yet, I would argue that the above explanation is not thorough enough. The 'sexual division of labour' does not take into account fully the persistence of the sexual dominance of men and the subordination of women. An explanation of the sexual division of labour must include an analysis of male power as well as the reasons for the subversion of women's species-producing power.

Power and the sexual division of labour

As we have seen, the sexual division of labour maintains an unwavering social importance, both theoretically and practically. Because of this presence, sexuality is given the power to define cultural value and social productivity. However, regardless of its power, sexuality is consistently made private or divorced from society. Sex/work, the private/the public, the family/society, work in the home/work in the factory, domestic labour/productive labour, reproduction/production and female/male are socially constructed opposites which relate directly to ideas about the sexual division of labour. These opposites conflict with each other. They also indicate the existence of a dominant sexual ideology. This ideology dictates that women should enact passive or subservient roles and be concerned with procreation, while men should live out dominant social roles and concern themselves with protection and providing for others.

Society believes that these respective roles are not only natural on the individual level but also morally correct on the social level. Thus, the goodness of any given society's sexual morality preserves itself in and through the continuance of the sexual division of labour and ultimately, the perpetuation of heterosexual roles.

Homosexuality vs the dominant sexual ideology

Homosexuality is the rejection of a traditional, dominant sexual ideology which, as we have seen, is heterosexual and male-orientated. Homosexuality is the practice of an alternative sexuality for either men or women. It is the concrete realization that some men aspire to practice 'social femininity', while some women desire to practice 'social masculinity'. Nicole Claude-Mathieu attempts to explain these categories when she says:

At the level of social norms of everyday life, 'social masculinity' is the unquestioned possibility of doing. It is responsibility. It is being numbered among the national heroes. 'Social femininity' is to be limited even before action is undertaken and when difficulty arises it is to turn to men. 'Social masculinity' is to know how to explain better, speak better, change wheels better and to hold out a hand to women when they run after the bus in a tight skirt and in four inch heels.[7]

Gay men are 'social females'. They tend to look to men for sexual and social support. Furthermore, they may establish close emotional ties with women, as women do among themselves. Lesbians are 'social males'. Contrary to popular myth they do not tend 'to hold out a hand to women who run after buses'. However, as a group, lesbians do tend to take up 'the unquestioned possibility of doing' or the practice of being productive. Possibly the following quotation may explain one reason for this tendency:

> Lesbians, on all levels, identify their interests with their jobs in a more concrete way than many women, since for them Prince Charming is not going to come galloping up and if, and when he does, he will be rejected. Lesbians seem frequently to take on extra work and responsibility; this fits in with their self-image, for capability and resourcefulness are necessarily desirable and attractive qualities in Lesbian life.[8]

Homosexuality upsets the dominant sexual ideology as well as confusing major issues like: 'Heterosexuality is ordained by nature'; 'Sex roles are natural and normal' or 'Masculine and feminine qualities are inherent in each sex'. Homosexuality denies the primacy of the family, as both an idea and an institution. As a result, the sexual division of labour becomes blurred.

Homosexuals, especially homosexual men, are generally viewed as 'a risk' in relation to their work role or productive function. For example, if a person's homosexuality is discovered in her/his work context, an individual may lose her/his job, not get promoted up the scale, experience discriminatory practice which affects her/his job performance, or be seen as a liability. It is almost as if homosexuality has a corrupting influence and heterosexuals are in danger of being contaminated by their presence.

As with sexuality in general, homosexuality is isolated and privatized. Yet, its existence is recognized and the fashioners of the dominant sexual ideology ask epidemiological questions such as: How do we cure this disease? or What accounts for its apparent spread? or etiological ones like: What are its causes? or How does one become a homosexual? Society tries to lock the closet door shut. Ultimately, it attempts to privatize homosexuality near to the point of possible extinction. One lesbian expressed the conviction that society does not uphold the viability of lesbian relationships. If it did, society would not only recognize these relationships, but also protect them:

> 'Lesbianism is not viable. It will never be viable until we're protected in our relationships with other women. If there's protection, there's privacy. However many people say, "What I do in bed is something between me and my partner", it's not true! This is because that very union threatens your whole way of life through jobs, family, etc. It isn't protected. Therefore, it's not private. So basically, your bed relationship is not valid. Although it isn't, it should be. . . . Being a lesbian is as valid as being a heterosexual. Society doesn't see this at the moment. No one asks a woman, "Are you a heterosexual?" No one asks that question. However, when the lesbian idea crops up, society heads straight for the bed scene.'

In a similar vein, society points an accusing finger at homosexuals and says: 'You're sexually sick and therefore, socially sick', 'You don't measure up to our standards'. The idea here is that homosexuals are socially sub-standard or individually diseased. The more liberal among us say, 'Sex is a private affair and I don't care what you do in bed.'

In a different vein, no one says to the homosexual, 'Sex is immanently social'; 'What you do sexually is interwoven with who you are in society and with what function you are to perform'; 'One's private life is really public'; 'The "sexual" is social' or 'The personal is political'.

The quandary remains and the choice for a 'meaningful' life is very limited.

> 'Instead of showing us our political potential, society tells us that we are something filthy, that we are over-sexed or that we are women trying to be pseudo-men. We're either sick or sinful. We have a physical maladjustment, a hormonal maladjustment or a mental maladjustment. In fact we are sexual and individual cripples. For them it's not worth beating around the bush.'

The rise of homosexual consciousness

Various social movements have emerged and have drawn attention to the social aspects of sexuality. As a result, homosexuality is viewed more as a cultural phenomenon and less as a unique sexual preference. Attempts are made to de-emphasize the 'sexual' or 'individual' elements of the 'disease' or 'problem' in favour of its social or even political implications. As one lesbian suggested, 'Sex isn't necessarily invisible. When it becomes conscious activity between people, it becomes visible and gains strength.'

New forms of consciousness are arising among sexual minority groups who are oppressed by the all-pervasive sexual ideology.[9] Today we are seeing this more and more.[10]

These new forms of consciousness may come to replace what were previous expressions of homosexual awareness. Historically, homosexuals tended to remain closeted. As a result, homosexual consciousness – one's awareness as a member of this oppressed minority – remained weak, very isolated, on an individual level or hidden from the mainstream of social life. I would term this type of awareness as 'pre-political' or lacking a group consciousness or solidarity with others.

Yes, homosexuals isolated themselves from society and each other. Who would blame them? A negative attitude, which was epitomized by the term 'crime against nature', developed in society towards homosexual practices. It is no wonder that most homosexuals denied themselves or were denied full access to society. However, this process still goes on today:

> 'If you are a homosexual, people are so shocked when you tell
> them. I rarely do until I know them. Potentially all people are
> shocked, but I suppose it depends upon how well you know them.
> When you tell them, they think of you as different from what they
> themselves are like. In fact, you're not that different. Well, I don't
> think that I am or else I wouldn't get on so well with straight
> people. In fact, I do because there are a lot of other parts to my
> personality.'

Society subverts any public expression of homosexual consciousness. Its attitudes stress the 'evil', 'sinful', 'sick' or 'individual' notion of homosexuality. These attitudes are detrimental not only to the development of political consciousness but also to an individual's self-worth or value.

'I was ashamed before. I am proud now.'

'I care very much what other people's views about lesbians are.
Because if they think when they meet me that lesbianism is awful
then I feel that this is quite wrong. They can dislike me as a person
but they shouldn't dislike me because of my lesbianism.'

Today homosexual politics represent a direct challenge to society.
The fight against sexual oppression is being waged on many fronts —
the individual and the social, the private and the public, and so on.
Terms like 'sexual politics',[11] 'sexism', 'male chauvinist', 'sexist',
'women's liberation' and 'gay' are now incorporated into everyday
jargon. Social movements which primarily criticize sexual oppression
have achieved varying degrees of public notice as well as support. It is
at this point in the discussion that the term 'social lesbianism' becomes
relevant.

The origins of social lesbianism

The development of lesbian politics or the birth of lesbianism as a social
movement has only recently become evident. Traditionally, any concern
for homosexuality revolved around men or male homosexuals. Lesbianism gained little credibility as a social phenomenon.[12] Its social relevance functioned primarily in the imaginations of men to titillate their
fantasies. Yet this image was marred by a rejection of acceptable
sexuality for women — if and when it became reality. Furthermore,
acceptable sexuality for women has always implied men for partners
as well as 'rule-creators'.

'I think it [lesbianism] is one of the most unacceptable ways of life
for a woman. Almost by definition a woman classifies herself
away from men. Also, it is different in that you almost have to
become something or someone different.'

'Men define you as a lesbian because you sleep with women. That's
all they think. So in fact you define yourself as a lesbian. Hopefully,
you have as little influences from outside sources as possible. As
soon as influence comes from society, you realize that it is
predominantly ruled by men. They're the ones who define you.'

It isn't chance that very few women in past generations had openly declared their homosexual feelings.[13] Confessed lesbian practice implied shame, stigma and possibly ostracism.[14] The closet was safer than open admission. At least, the closet helped an individual lesbian to 'legitimate' or justify her 'deviant' label on a personal level. Needless to say, the hidden life subverted a social critique of lesbianism.

> 'My ideas of lesbianism have changed. I saw it as a dirty, twisted, ghastly thing that I had done. It was an experience that I couldn't tell anybody about. And yet, it felt so good and the emotions were so marvellous. It was a hell of a muddle.'

> 'I thought that my first experience was just a one-off. I had fallen very much in love and been loved tremendously by a woman and that was it. However, the second time around lasted nine years and involved many elements. I was moving into gay politics and then lesbian politics. I found that lesbianism wasn't just bed! It was interwoven with the needs of women and the status of women too.'

Historically, it seems as if there have always been 'lesbian ghettos', what I would describe as pockets of social activity which were characterized by intense emotional and sexual relationships between women. Whether or not we know about the ill-fated island of Lesbos and its renowned inhabitant Sappho, the Greek lyric poetess who set up a school for girls and a cult for lesbians, we should be aware that this type of ghetto existed during the early sixth century BC. In *The Well of Loneliness*,[15] Radclyffe Hall, a lesbian novelist, alludes to a similar ghetto which emerged in Paris during the first part of this century.

Traditionally, lesbian ghettos may have existed as socially designated areas for those engaged in unapproved activities or as what sociologists term 'sub-cultures of deviance'. In these contexts, lesbian consciousness remains dormant. It is politically insipid. Social lesbianism counteracts this state. Through it, lesbianism gains momentum as a social force and becomes a political potential for women.

Social lesbianism: a new consciousness

As stated above, social lesbianism manifests itself as a new form of consciousness which is emerging for women. In this way, it becomes a source of strength and establishes an important link between one's experience as a woman and a lesbian.

'I see myself first as a lesbian or as a woman. Now to me the two are almost synonymous, so I just feel very whole I suppose. I feel myself. I mean I don't feel at one with society, but I'm beginning to feel more real, more strong than I have ever done before . . . which is really exciting.'

'Lesbianism is still an emotive word. Yet, it does describe what it means to be a woman, a woman-identified-woman and a woman-loving-woman. It filters right out into the things that really upset women about being women. That is that they are unable to be the same.'

'The lesbian identity is woman and I'm thinking more and more that I'm less and less a lesbian and more and more a woman. I find the two labels so interrelated – whereas before I thought being a lesbian was a totally separate thing than being a woman.'

In other words lesbianism has the potential to become political when it actively exposes the tensions between sexual practice and society or between a private notion of sex and a public conception of sexuality between men and women in patriarchy/capitalism. It also makes visible those problems which exist between women's productive role, which appears to be minimal, and women's reproductive role, which, although important for the continuance of society, is under-estimated.

This book will emphasize that lesbianism is a complex and changing social fact. As a social construction, lesbianism implies a variety of interactions for a woman in society. She changes not only as the networks of lesbian activity expand and grow into more socially recognizable forms but also with the development of social lesbianism. In effect, it may transform dominant ideas about the sexual and women's role or social function. Resistant to these dominant ideas, groups create alternative forms of sexual practice. They present a direct challenge to the monolithic structure of the sexual. Because lesbians are oppressed by the ways in which society organizes sexuality into rigid roles, they are able to develop a unique consciousness as lesbian women.

As a result, contemporary lesbians, whom this study is about, need not remain isolated in the closet as did their predecessors. Many are emerging from the privacy of their cocoons in order to confront society. The metamorphosis occurs when public declarations of their newfound awareness are made. Yet, contradictory feelings still remain for some.

> 'I feel right out of society because I don't like it anyways not just because I am a lesbian. I mean in real terms *it* [society] is a counter-culture. I feel strongly that ours could be a predominant culture but then I think how much I am living in cloud cuckoo land. How many other people in counter-groups think that they are just or it's just a short time before they come to fruition? All sorts of small groups feel that. The point is that it [society] is growing so fast that you just can't pretend any more.'

Social lesbianism becomes the key to opening the closet door. Through this impetus as a social force, lesbians don't have to 'pretend any more'; they are able to be themselves.

Remember that ideas about homosexuality — therefore, lesbianism — are consistent with society's attitudes towards sexuality in general. These attitudes uphold 'essentialism', which is the view that sexuality or sexual practice is 'an essence', 'a part of human nature' or 'inherent'. Homosexuals and heterosexuals alike suffer from the oppressive features of essentialism. In other words, the sexual is viewed as having to do with a permanent characteristic which is grounded in one's biological make-up. It is fixed and unchanging. If one is born a woman, one should *be* a woman or 'female'. The same applies to a man. Culture influences 'it' (sexuality) in a marginal or minor way. The social construction of sexuality is ruled out! Social lesbianism as a group force negates essentialism; yet, individual 'social lesbians' may uphold this view. Thus, contradictions are ever-present in the realm of the sexual, the social, the personal and the political.

'Sick, but not sorry' lesbians and 'Sorry, but we're not sick' lesbians

The above views compel some women to treat their lesbianism as a 'fixed entity', 'something they're stuck with for life' or a 'purely sexual thing'. Usually, however, these lesbians admit that their lesbian practice grew from emotional relationships with women. They contradict themselves. On the one hand, lesbianism is a purely sexual *thing*. On the other hand, lesbian feelings are not necessarily sexual but always include strong ties with women.

'I had no choice in the matter, but it is a commitment to women. It is basically inherent.'

'My lesbianism hasn't really changed. I have always accepted myself. I've always had crushes on women. Immediately, I accepted this. People used to say, "Well, there is a name for people like you!" I used to think, "Bloody idiot, there isn't at all." This was because I knew that my feelings weren't at all sexual. The fact that they became so when I was fifteen was just something different. But, I was never really upset about how people would react. I have always been strong-minded about it and pleased when I sorted out what I was.'

'Social lesbians' — those lesbians who are involved in some form of group awareness — who express the above attitudes are what I would term the 'sick, but not sorry' type ('sorry' in this context refers to regret; the colloquialism, 'I beg your pardon', refers to the other type). In varying degrees they placidly accept traditional lesbian images. In this way, they collude with the dominant sexual ideology. Yet, ironically, they do not regret their 'infirmity' or 'condition'. They accept their lesbianism as a fact in their lives. In reality, they appear to enjoy 'it' as they meet others in the social context of bars, clubs, and discos.

As a group, they reveal some interesting social practices. On one level, not only are their social lives ghettoized (removed from the mainstream of social life) but also they lend deaf ears to any discussion of lesbian politics. On another level, by coming somewhat out of the closet, they break down a rigid historical tradition and unconsciously further the 'lesbian cause'. Thus, a contradiction between a personal life and a political life is present. This presence is most probably evidence of a 'pre-political' stage of lesbian consciousness. In other words, it is the point before which lesbianism achieves recognition as a social force and becomes a political movement. At this stage it seems socially impotent. Yet, regardless of this apparent weakness, it is political. By the very fact that this practice actively questions social norms, and ultimately challenges society itself, it contributes to a new understanding of sexuality, if not lesbianism.

Another group of social lesbians, the 'sorry, but we're not sick' type, furthers this critique of society. They not only come out of the closet but they go out into the streets. They are neither sick nor sorry for being lesbians and they tend to appear as an oppressed minority.

On the one hand, this group polarizes the sexual and social definitions of both lesbians and women. In other words, they point out the necessity of questioning 'social femininity' for women. 'Sexual being' does not equal 'woman'. On the other hand, while upholding the importance of being a woman, they do not act in a way which is acceptable for a woman. For them, lesbianism is not primarily a sexual practice and women are not primarily sexual creatures who exist for men's pleasure. Lesbianism is a commitment to women in a male-dominated society. Furthermore, all women have the potential to be lesbians. This belief is their ultimate threat to society.

'I suppose I see the lesbian as being one who stands up to all who don't want to be defined by their roles. I suppose that's why we are so persecuted because men are afraid of women who can live independently of them.'

'I used to think of lesbians as women who had sex with other women but now I don't think that this is crucial. I think it's a question of being physical with women but it's not the sex.'

'Lesbianism is that I have a feeling with other women – a feeling of empathy and putting them first and relating to them on a primary level, rather than in a secondary way (in the usual way that women relate to other women or in the way that men relate to us generally). And yet, men are usually their primary relationships and I suppose I have changed my views. I don't see it [lesbianism] in purely sexual terms.'

'As a lesbian, you totally reject the heterosexual way of living and you look upon your relationships as being with women. In other words, you count men out of it all together. Not that you can't be friends with a man, but you take a friendship only so far with a man, then, it stops. This happens normally when the sexual part of a relationship comes into it. You can become close friends with a man but the moment when there is some sexual involvement, you back off. Then, you just associate yourself with women. At that

point in time, you can only associate closely with women. There is
no way in which you can see yourself with a man. Whether you
have in the past doesn't matter. You've decided you're a lesbian
and a lesbian must totally commit herself to women.

Within either a reform or a revolutionary movement, social lesbians
may link their oppression with others. Within many of these movements, the 'sexual' relates to the 'political'. Sexual oppression may be
experienced on many levels — in terms of general male and female
roles, alternative child-rearing, shared parental responsibility for children in the domestic scene, men as househusband, etc. — not just on the
level of sexual preference as with homosexuals or bisexuals. Interestingly
enough, lesbians may experience further oppression as women in male-
dominated gay organizations, as either gay, or women in the radical
left, or as lesbians in the women's movement. Possibly, one of their
political functions in these oppressive contexts is to expose contradictions between theory (what one abstractly knows) and practice (what
one does). These groups are obviously oppressive. Yet, they purport to
be 'politically aware' or to maintain 'the true consciousness'. In reality,
false consciousness runs rampant. It may be that this latter type of
consciousness is really a particular group's or movement's imitation
of the dominant sexual ideology which is primarily male, heterosexual-
orientated.

In light of the above, some lesbians discussed their feelings:

'I suppose what groups you join depends or I think it's in terms of
how you view your perspective on society, whether it's in line with
who has the power and who hasn't and the power relationships that
it produces . . . also, it's in terms of seeing yourself as living under a
patriarchal structure which affects one's life really severely . . . .
Well, that's what it means for me anyways . . . . As a woman, society
restricts me and this doesn't mean that if you're a lesbian you will
see it in this way.'

'I am a person who derives strength from the group context. I had a
leap in consciousness when I joined International Socialists then I
joined Gay Liberation Front . . . . Then, I left it to join a
consciousness-raising group. I've never been a lesbian outside of a
movement. I've come out and never really had a period in the closet.
I gained strength in the group context.'

'When GLF started I knew immediately that I had to go to the first meeting. I didn't even think about it. I felt really at home there in the group environment. It did fantastic things for me. Yet, it was very male-dominated and the women were always separated.'

'In any movement one hears of these awful stories. I think of one of these CHE [Campaign for Homosexual Equality] groups where the men take it for granted that the women are going to go back-stage and make the coffee and all this business. I know it's a trivial example but, my god, it's every minute of your life. So I think every woman has got to take much more of a part. . . . I mean we are not equal. We are not equal in anyone's eyes except perhaps a few.'

'I think for a while I was very much on a limb because initially in the women's movement one couldn't talk about lesbianism. It was very, very tough. But, other women were so frightened by it – we [lesbians] couldn't talk about ourselves. We were all so scared that the women's liberation movement would be branded as a load of lesbians that we did not talk about it with straight women. I felt so repressed by all of this.'

'I wanted very much to be active in the women's movement but I saw the lesbian problem as being a crucial part of it. Lesbians were, in the beginning anyways, denied any validity. Then of course, things got much better. Now it's possible to have the perspective of lesbians being totally linked up with women's liberation.'

'I felt so oppressed by IS [International Socialists] when they told me, "You must not tell working-class women that you are a lesbian.'

Social lesbianism – a dialectic[16]

As we have seen briefly, both types of social lesbian polarize ideas on lesbianism and sexuality. They point out how lesbianism has developed from an individual experience to a social one and from a totally closeted environment to a relatively 'out' life-style.

Previously, we discussed the dynamics of power and the sexual division of labour. Lesbianism illuminates the above discussion. In the light of the sexual division of labour and its relationship to women, as a social group, lesbianism drives a wedge between the role to reproduce and the role to produce, women's primary function in society and women's secondary function or women as reproducers and women as producers. Its very existence causes this opposition. Furthermore, in society's eyes, lesbianism minimizes women's role to reproduce in favour of a productive role which is usually reserved for men. Many lesbians desire economic independence from a man. As a result, their jobs may become very important to them.

A labour force which provides a better bargaining position as well as a greater potential for organization may be emerging for women and for lesbians. It is interesting to point out that in this sample of social lesbians, 49 per cent of the total sample were included in the three highest occupational levels: Higher Managerial or Professional, Lower Managerial or Professional and Skilled or Supervisory. Perhaps these lesbians are included in the group of women who

> have been drawn into the greatly expanded, further and higher educational system, encouraged through that process to expect equal job opportunity with men and able, subsequently, to get sufficiently highly paid employment to remain economically independent of marriage.[17]

Also lesbians are biologically women or structurally 'females' and culturally 'men' or 'social males'. In society's view they have the biological potential to reproduce, whether they use it or not. Society's vision is blurred because as 'social males', lesbians should not reproduce. Yet some lesbians do.

For most women this biological potential becomes a reality in the traditional family unit which exists primarily for procreation. This happens when a legal contract transforms itself into a permanent sexual relationship with a specific man, a husband. Lesbians have a tendency to reject both the structure of the family and the husband-wife relationship. Ultimately, a lesbian may deny motherhood. Because motherhood is usually attainable only through the traditional heterosexual family, society denies it for her.[18]

As women, lesbians experience society's command to be dependent upon men for protection and money. The husband's wage is a symbol of this dependency and it characterizes women's relationship to money in advanced capitalist societies.

It becomes evident that this position (lesbianism) rejects the family structure as well as traditional forms of power. As a social force, it contradicts social values and society. Previously it was stated that lesbians are viewed as being 'social males' by society. Yet within the general category 'male' or in relationship to men they are not primarily productive (viewed as workers). Also, in relationship to women as a social group or to 'structural females', which lesbians are as well, they do not become visible as primarily reproductive (viewed as mothers). This ambivalent state contributes to making lesbianism a distinct social category which is isolated and divorced from meaningful social life and which appears as politically impotent. In a state of confusion and fear, society wants to get rid of lesbianism. It utilizes 'scare tactics'. It tells men that lesbians are competing for 'their women'. (Thus far, society hasn't seen how they compete for 'their jobs'.) In reality, however, the lesbian struggle is for women's liberation – and the struggles of all people against sexual and economic oppression.

To summarize, lesbianism presents a twofold challenge to women's position: (1) By seeking economic independence from men, by not entering into the marriage situation or by not remaining in the marriage contract, lesbians threaten women's traditional relationship to money through the male wage (husband's income). (2) By experiencing an alternative sexual practice for women, lesbians defy the dominant sexual ideology. Its very existence proves that it is not necessary for women to have sex with men, that women do not have to be 'sexy' or primarily 'sexual' in order to survive as women and that lesbianism may have more to do with power and how it is distributed in society than was previously considered.

Social lesbianism may not substantially alter the position of women in society. However, it actively calls into question traditional social attitudes towards women as being primarily reproductive, as 'colonized' within the home and as sexually orientated towards men. As a force, social lesbianism is a contradiction to sexuality in society and a potential threat to the basis of all social relationships in that society.

2 The social reality of lesbianism

'Lesbianism is a total way of life in the sense that it's like being born again. I mean that's how I feel. The trouble is though, the old me didn't die completely. There's still lots of crap left over from the old life and so one's born again and literally that's how I feel now living with all these wonderful women. But, I also got lots of shit and conditioning from my old life which still hangs on.'

'Lesbianism colours your whole life, it has to. You're slightly cut off from society in general and you don't talk about it openly. I mean people come in and say, I mean the people at work mainly about their husbands, I mean they come in all red-eyed and weeping saying, "The bastard's left me and ain't it awful, darling" . . . . But you can't come in red-eyed and weeping and say, "My girl-friend has played me up." So this is why I say up to a point you are cut off.'

'It's just the way it is, like when I brush my teeth, when I breathe, that's a lesbian breathing . . . it's a total way of life because I'm a lesbian twenty-four hours a day even when I'm on the street, but I don't walk around and say, "Hey, look I'm a lesbian." '

'It's total, complete, but it's shared with heterosexuals. I mean let's face it. Our parents are heterosexuals. I'm certainly not one of those people who would like to see them off the face of the earth. How crazy can one get. I have many het friends as I have lesbian or male homosexual friends . . . . It's unreal the same way that if you're wholly with hets you get hangups because there are certain things where we don't relate even in conversations. You take a lesbian in hairdressers, for example, they're all yapping around about babies and food and cooking and that kind of thing.'

'I think we have a total way of life and possibly far more intellect in a way, probably because some of us have suffered even if it was only the growing realization of what you are. I think we should mix with all people – the more the better, while we can educate people as I flatter myself as I have done. That's why I have a pretty easy life as far as being a lesbian is concerned because I just made them understand. There is no good trying to fight people. Persuasion, that's the answer, and understanding.'

These feelings convey lesbianism as being both a personal awareness and a way of life. Consistent with the above, society's conception of lesbianism reflects a sense that lesbianism remains a particular isolated feeling, an unusual way of life or both.

Earlier I indicated that for lesbians a transition is occurring. I termed this development social lesbianism. Here the implication is that it becomes more group-orientated, 'institutionalized' or structured as a specific life-style or 'sub-culture'. Various social groups form and make claims to 'lesbian consciousness'.

In turn society not only denies this consciousness on the group level but often condemns these feelings when they are experienced on the individual level. This chapter is concerned with the latter aspect, while Chapter 3 describes the former. In an immediate sense, the present chapter stands apart from the major content of the book in that by describing lesbian identity and lesbian relationships, it appears to give priority to the individual over and above the group context. However, as we shall see, the isolated person is never really divorced from that context and this chapter does lend fluidity to the development of the perspective set out in the book.

The lesbian identity and women – a difference?

One's identity becomes meaningful *only* as one becomes aware of who one is in relationship to others. Identity necessitates 'social identity' and usually determines the nature and scope of one's involvement in society. It requires both solitary and shared experiences. For the lesbian, her identity exists as a 'counter-identity' which challenges directly a society based on male-orientated heterosexual relations. It is an identity contrary to what is expected of *all* women.

A lesbian knows that her life is different from that of other women.

This perception brings with it a certain amount of negativity. What are the implications which arise within the lesbian perspective? How do these affect one's identity as a woman? What does a 'counter-identity' mean and how is it experienced?

As we forge ahead into a relatively new field of thought, we will answer these questions and, I hope, we will expand our own interest. Three areas are important for our understanding:

1   The lesbian way of life as an unacceptable one for women.
2   A lesbian life-style as less restricted and freer than those of the majority of women.
3   A lesbian identity as a counter-identity.

First, a lesbian way of life is not an acceptable one for women. Society views women as having sexual relationships with men, regardless of the fact that their emotional relationships may or may not be consistent with this view. Furthermore, lesbians, defined primarily within the former area of relationships, suffer not only from an 'oversexed' image but also an unacceptable one.

'Immediately, when society thinks of us, they think it's the sex bit.'

'Once I told a man, "I am not a total sex creature or out to sleep with every woman I meet. I live a normal life. You may have a prick and think I do, but I don't. I don't have one, need one or want one. Furthermore, I don't have to think with one like you do." He looked at me with utter amazement.'

Objectively, lesbians do not meet up to society's standards for women and they do not fit into the proper social category which society ordains for them. As far as society is concerned, they remain 'deviant'.

'They think all sorts of things . . . perverts, abominable mutations . . . . We had arguments with a woman who told us that we were abominable mutations . . . but I don't think that I can find anything perverse or deviant about women, they are beautiful whole people.'

'Society, zilch . . . . Society views us very badly. I think society doesn't realize that it's a threat and therefore, just thinks of it as sick and disgusting . . . and unnatural. But it doesn't know the reason why and doesn't bother to think why it should be.'

'I think it's one of the very much unacceptable ways of life for a woman. Almost by definition a woman, a lesbian classifies herself away from men. We're all different in that you are something different . . . . So men define you as a lesbian and you define yourself as a lesbian and you define the way you live as a lesbian. You get some feedback from society because it's ruled predominantly by men.'

Other lesbians point out that society is really uneducated, blind or ignorant in its understanding:

'I think that general society or the wider society is uneducated because it thinks lesbians are queer in some sense or very odd . . . . Maybe they think we're very off-putting. I presume I don't like society's way of life because I'm afraid to come right out and say without being pushed into it, "I'm a lesbian", and I wouldn't dream of introducing it into the conversation.'

'Society takes a poor view of lesbianism out of ignorance. I think that they think that we are poor and frustrated. They're unnatural and they are women who can't get themselves a man, you know, that kind of thing. I'm not talking about sophisticated society, but if you were to take a whole spectrum of the 20 million adults that there are in England, it's even worse than being single, I think, which is at least excusable because poor thing at least she couldn't get a man.'

Some feel that society's views are changing:

'I suppose society's attitudes are changing and getting much better. Whereas it used to be taboo and revolting and all that there's much more of it on TV and in the movies. Wherever you turn lesbianism is talked about, so soon it will be much more of an accepted thing.'

'We're in the middle of a big change. Yes, it used to be considered "deviant" and it probably will for a long time but much less so. It's changing rapidly in leaps and bounds. What else is there to say?'

From the above, we see that lesbians feel, know and experience that their lives are different from other women and, ultimately, from social expectations. Yet they have chosen and continually choose to live this difference.

Second, a lesbian life-style appears less restricted and freer than most women's. Women exist as 'servants' or 'carers' for men.

'In a society which regards men of primary importance to women, lesbians are unlucky. Society thinks, "Poor things, they haven't got any men to cope with or care for." '

'I think, or rather certainly if a woman doesn't exist to serve a man, she doesn't exist. And to have a satisfactory existence on her own is unthinkable and threatening. One of the very amusing things to me was that lesbians can move quite comfortably together in society and not be recognized because it's not recognized that women exist independently of men.'

In addition, all women should be the bearers of their children and should produce as 'female' labourers, a secondary workforce. Most women, as individuals, service one man or a series of men in the family set-up. Lesbians, whether married or not or whether mothers or not, have the potential to go beyond these functions and to become independent women:

'Lesbianism is open and the rest of them are closed little boxes. I mean basically you can open a door, I mean you can open a refrigerator door and stay in there. You walk into it and you stay right there. OK? Other ways of life are not particularly open. They're shut. I mean everything else is a stereotype that you can walk into.'

Objectively, lesbians loosen the chains which bind women to the legalities of marriage and the restrictions of family life. As workers outside the domestic context, lesbians, like other women in this area, emphasize a more productive, work-orientated role. In order to exist these women have to create an alternative. (Contrary to society's view, many working wives don't just bring in pin-money when they go out to work. In England women make up 40 per cent of the workforce.) Yet, ironically, for lesbians this situation creates an atmosphere of relative freedom in comparison with other women who are bound to husbands and children:

'I suspect we may be freer to make what we want of our lives economically independent of men. Yes, I mean we presumably, most of us, have to look after ourselves financially. Therefore, we've got a certain amount of financial independence as well as a certain amount of emotional independence. Well, I think one is freer than the average straight woman is into the nuclear family. I think one can carve out one's own parameters, perimeters or whatever.'

'We are very much against the assumptions of heterosexuality that exist in society, of being a wife and mother, of being financially dependent. We're certainly up against what all women are. I think what it is is that we are nearer to a person than, as it were, a category. So you can act as a person and God willing you're free to act as a person, true to yourself with any luck and that might strike some people as a bit odd.'

'An awful lot of people in the world are terribly tied. We have got a freedom, if we take it, of being true to ourselves as women and not to ourselves as lesbians. I am what I am you know so to the extent that we are capable of being free we are going against all standard pictures of ourselves as women or which is rather idealistic, but I think that's what it could be and what in the good moments it is.'

Third, the lesbian identity is a counter-identity. On the face of it, when a lesbian interacts with society, she is usually considered to be a 'normal' heterosexual women. Yet she is not; she is a lesbian. Whether she is open about it or not, she may experience a wide range of negative reactions or social approbation — from slight awkwardness in herself, others or both; embarrassment; uneasiness; outright rudeness; rejection or 'snubbing' from others. The potential for negativity creates an almost 'in-built' awareness of her 'deviant identity', 'different choice' or alternative life-style. However, this negative feature of her identity does not alter her commitment to women. Rather, it reveals the oppressive characteristics of the dominant sexual ideology which is expressed in social interactions.

'Lesbianism — it's just not on for them.'

'We're just freaks or kinky women.'

'All of my life, I've felt oppressed, but why? Am I weird or something?'

'Why is it there is always horror or fear about us? In the beginning I was scared but I know there is nothing terrible about us, nothing any more terrible than anyone else.'

Some lesbians say that not only is lesbianism a counter-identity but also women's identity is a counter-identity in a male-orientated society. What does this mean?

'Women, I think women are second-class citizens.'

'Women don't exist. Only men exist.'

'I suppose I see a lesbian as one who stands up for all women who don't want to be defined by their roles. That's why we're so persecuted because men are afraid of women who can live independently. We are a counter-identity, but it's not the single identity for women. There are many types of identities as there are within every group in society. We're trying to show that women exist.'

'Women are so oppressed that I can see only the beginnings of what I would call a woman's identity. Before the women's movement you couldn't even say what or who women were because they are so much tied up with and defined by men.'

From the above explanation we should be able to see the implications of lesbianism for an individual. An additional aspect of this experience is the creation of façades or fronts in the social arena. A lesbian may embrace either a 'closeted' life-style or an 'out' life-style. 'Closeted' refers to a way of life in which she keeps hidden the fact that she is a lesbian. The 'out' type is more open and through it she tends to admit, or should we say proclaim, her lesbianism. However, we must keep in mind that a spectrum of life-styles exists rather than a sharp polarity. A lesbian's movement along this spectrum (degree of openness or closetedness) is dependent upon a variety of factors — whom she is with, where she is, how she feels.

The closet life

The reality of the closet reveals that not only relationships, but also a way of life are consistently hidden, privatized or isolated. The closet is familiar to all lesbians at some point in their lives. Yet, as I implied earlier, its door is observable as having varying degrees of openness or 'closedness', as the case may be, from locked shut to partially open, to almost totally open to open wide.

In the closet, a lesbian hides her intimate relationships with women.

'Most people don't know. There are a lot of people that I feel would not be able to accept it, hence I back away from telling them, which I'm sure is wrong.'

'I don't think it's worth it. I don't think it's necessary to give people a problem if it may help my way of life, anyways it won't help their way of life, it will only create confusion and give them a problem to be accepted on that basis or not to be. It's not going to help my problems, in the end it may help society's though.'

'How much is it going to affect what you are doing at the moment? Now, if I were to make it public knowledge at work, say, that then means how much do I care about my job? How much am I willing to lay on the line the fact that my personal life is such and such? I have relationships with other women. How important is that in comparison with my work? Am I willing to take the consequences at work just to make something public knowledge which is private?'

'If I were having a relationship with a man I wouldn't tell many people so I don't tell people or go out of my way to tell people something which could affect my career prospects.'

'I don't feel that there is any reason to let them know what is going on with me. Maybe, if I told them it could have repercussions somewhere.'

These lesbians allow others to believe that they are heterosexual. This deliberate silence upholds the dominant sexual ideology which is the ultimate cause of their silence. By taking upon themselves in public situations a role which is inconsistent with their private lives, they reflect a living contradiction. Goffman calls this 'role distance',[1] although he doesn't refer specifically to lesbians, because a lesbian is unable to encompass the role of a straight woman. In other words, if she implies or moreover states that she is straight, she appears as distant from lesbianism. Yet, in reality, by encompassing lesbianism as a way of life, she effectively removes herself from active involvement in a straight woman's role.

> 'Now the big generality of people in my life don't know. They may have the sense to work it out but I don't suppose it would ever cross their minds. I think not. They must think I'm straight, so I let them.'

Thus, a contradiction is evident. A privatized life, made so by an individual and society, remains hidden under the surface. The creation of very well defined boundaries between an individual's private life and public life, personal and political, is effected. While a pivotal reality for oneself, lesbianism becomes a secret life and hidden from others.

> 'I just don't know, some of them might think it or guess. I drop little hints. I only know two people who positively know about me — my doctor and my boss, but others might guess. My family know, my two sisters and their husbands. My parents must have guessed because they see —— [lover's name] and the flat and the double bed in the bedroom. I presume they must have leaped to a few conclusions. Anyone who does seem to know it makes no difference. I mean they seem either pleased that I'm happy as it were or it doesn't enter into it.'

However, in some cases conscious subversion transforms 'a secret life' into a seemingly 'open' heterosexual life-style: 'I take great pains to hide it. I even make up names of boyfriends or male lovers so that I have a cover.' This façade blocks any social understanding as well as negating any form of individual consciousness or answers to questions like, 'Why does my oppression exist?' Thus the closet makes one unable to challenge publicly society's views. Society wins out. The dominant ideology remains intact and perhaps, it gathers more power. 'Ideology makers' or those who hold this power gain support, knowingly or unknowingly, from the closeted lesbian: 'The justification for the closet varies from lesbian to lesbian'; 'Lesbians are seen as sick, evil . . . and coming out will cause people to get upset', or 'Why should I tell people, if they'll only treat me differently – like some sort of freak?'

Lesbians afraid of coming out feel that they may be rejected by others. I would contend that this fear of rejection is one of the primary reasons for the maintenance of the closet life-style. Other related reasons are fear of being seen as 'sick', 'evil', 'deviant', 'emotionally unstable', etc.; guilt because one is and continues to be an 'unacceptable' person; desire to maintain the status quo: not to upset others unduly; for the convenience of not having to explain one's life to others and to avoid embarrassment whether at work, with straight friends or family.

'I don't think it's worth it. I want friends to accept me.'

'I just don't tell people because it's none of their business and why – to let them have something against me?'

'When the subject of men comes up, I just shy away. My workmates or friends might know. I don't want to embarrass them and lose their friendship.'

From the above, we see that the closet causes the lesbian to create a false self which she presents to others. Undercurrents of suspicion from others combined with her own self-denial or even self-hatred do affect her self-image. For some, the effects are disastrous:

'I wanted to kill myself when I became a lesbian. I felt trapped and bound to a life hidden from everything. I felt as if I couldn't cope.'

'When I was in the closet, I was totally paranoid. I thought all of the time someone was going to do me in. I guess mainly because of the things I was involved in. I mean they were terrible, well as far as society was and is concerned.'

'I used to get so depressed because I wasn't free to be myself.'

'Once, I tried to kill myself.'

The out life

To be open about one's lesbianism reveals a certain amount of consciousness. The 'out' lesbian is aware that her public declarations do challenge society and social norms. She explicitly defies them by defining herself in a social group which appears as unacceptable and which is contrary to women's function in society. Yet, in spite of these factors, a lesbian finds a sense of security which is maintained by the support and encouragement she receives from others.

> 'Lots of women, even me up until very recently, didn't like it [lesbianism] . I didn't like it. I wished that I could change. Before I came out, I wished I could have been straight so that I didn't have to face that problem, and to have that stick with which all of society could beat me with. But now I could no more think of being straight than fly. It just doesn't figure. I have hassles still in my head, particularly with my mother. I don't realize how that freaked me out still. I just want to learn fast . . . when we were walking back from — [a friend's name] there were two girls playing all sorts of games and I said, "Thank God". I mean we muck about but I know we don't play games – that's a conspiracy of silence. With others I have become strong enough to help to break it down.'

> 'When I came out I told everyone that I was gay. I expected a lot of hostility but all the women were fascinated by it. They all kept ringing me up and wanted to see me. They were fascinated.'

> 'Coming out can be very positive. My relationship with my mother is very close now.'

A lesbian may also sense that she has a newfound awareness or strength from challenging society:

> 'Perverse. I cannot see how a physical manifestation of something can be seen as perverse. To me it's one of the most beautiful things and if someone says it's sick, or evil or depraved, I just cannot associate with it. Yet, I am associated with it constantly. I'm strong now because I reject these ideas.'

'Being a lesbian for me involves being a feminist and putting women first. I lead a lesbian life-style holding hands in the street. You have to learn how to develop a very thick skin when people make remarks and that means drawing strength from yourself as a woman. To say, "Fuck you, I don't need you" or "You think this is where I'm at". I don't care and I think that kind of thing is very important. We need women who are strong, independent and don't mind being open.'

Or she may find that a transformation in her self-image and support system has occurred:

'I'm proud now; I was ashamed before. I am open and find others who are too.'

'Now I do look more to my friends for support and I feel less isolated.'

Some lesbians refer to being 'out' as an experience of a new life which appears to bring more happiness than before:

'You've got so much crap. I'd say that what I've learned in the last year has been the only thing which is relevant to me. For the past 27 years, I've had all that crap put into me. I feel like I'm a toddler, a new baby just learning . . . I mean even now all those times when you might think or act in an old sort of way, it doesn't work. This is the way I act even with my mother.'

'The fact that I've decided that I'm a lesbian, which by the way I don't mind being a lesbian. There are positive benefits for me in being one. It is simply a process of coming to terms with myself and it's a growing-up process even if I'm already 45.'

'I'm much happier now. I'm at last doing what I'm meant to be doing and whereas before I was kidding myself, I was playing a role that wasn't me. Even though I didn't know what was wrong, I knew there was something wrong. I knew I wasn't doing the things that I was supposed to be doing or what I should be doing. Most important how I should be doing it.'

'I'm much more confident as a lesbian. I didn't have any confidence before. I mean I'm getting so that I could explain to others whilst before I couldn't in a month of Sundays. I still find it difficult to explain it to someone who isn't a lesbian. I can put it into words much better. You know the whys and the wherefores and how it isn't dirty and disgusting, how it has a lot of political significance and how open it is or can be.'

Lesbians find support or encouragement from those who do not consider lesbianism as an indicator of 'badness' in a person. Some say that others tend to accept them if they have knowledge of them as good persons or friends.

'For some people it is worth telling them. It is worth it to get my point over to friends of long standing where there is a good relationship going and I am sure they accept it and it doesn't affect their reaction to me. They know me and like me anyway.'

However, this is not always true and some people with whom one shares a close relationship may be threatened or cut off altogether:

'My mother was appalled. I suppose that's the only way to describe it at all. She gives me a very hard time still. I tried to see her and help her through it because I think it's something which I think she needed, support. But she just gave me a hard time. I wrote to her about three or four days ago and said, "I can't handle what you're doing to me. I love you dearly, I always have done. I always will but you can't put me down all of the time. I can't handle it, so I'm not going to see you for a while." She sent me a bunch of flowers, when she got that letter. I thought it was really nice. So I think that perhaps she is beginning to realize that it's not something shameful or so vile.'

'I never saw — again after I told her I was a lesbian.'

Through friends, she develops a network of relationships which cushion her from the blows of stigma, shame or guilt and which help her to come out. Furthermore, coming out implies that she is 'strong enough' to begin to cope with these 'blows'.

Recalling her coming out, one lesbian said: 'I was so afraid to come out. And yet, after I did I felt that it was one of the easiest things to do in my life.' Later, I discovered that what accounted for this ease was the support she received from a close-knit women's group in which she was an active member.

Consistently, my study revealed that a lesbian, whether closeted or not, recognized the dominance of the heterosexual male ideology which oppressed her. She knew that society views her life as 'deviant' and that there is a 'sub-culture' into which society slots her.

Furthermore, I would contend that in order for her life to be lived out effectively as a challenge to society a lesbian would become involved in co-operative social activity or collective social action. The out lifestyle lends itself to this challenge. If a lesbian rejects the group experience and remains totally closeted, she may become fraught with isolation, frustration and fear.

One lesbian spoke about how for many years she had been isolated. Her life was characterized by total dependence upon her lover as well as fear:

'I never met another lesbian besides —. She was the only lesbian that I knew. I was fearful of meeting others. Gradually, I saw that I had to talk to other lesbians about my feelings, my problems which I had because of my guilt. I began to go places where other lesbians met [clubs and bars]. They were just ordinary people like myself. I was shocked in a way. I thought they'd be like what I read in books.'

This lesbian emerged from her cocoon of isolation only to discover that others like herself had similar experiences. Isolation breaks down as the positive rewards of an 'open' life outweigh the negative effects of a hidden life. Thus, individual consciousness is linked up with others and one's life becomes 'de-privatized' or less secluded. As an alternative, the out life may supply meaning to the secretiveness or possible terror of one's past.

On the one hand, if a lesbian defines herself as sick, deviant, maladjusted, etc., she will not view her lesbianism as a meaningful alternative which has the potential to develop with others. She may hide her 'sickness' in the closet. On the other hand, if this alternative is chosen, it implicitly binds one to a group identity or awareness which attempts to create a new lesbian image by openly challenging society. The conscious or unconscious target is visibility with others.

One area in which this visibility may or may not be maintained is at work. Openness may mean losing one's job:

> 'Before I came out, I left work in the evening and became a lesbian in a sense. It was impossible for me to say, "I am a lesbian." But now I'm a lesbian all of the time. It didn't do me much good – I got the sack.'

Being out may also be the source of unwarranted humour in one's job:

> 'At work I'm as out as one can be without being an exhibitionist. I don't wear badges which is what some others do. But I have made it clear to members of staff. It's difficult at work because at times you're pushed into being a figure of fun. They cope with you making everything you say as outrageous. So you start playing ball with them. So when my bike was stolen, I said, "How could I be a dyke on a bike if I don't have a bike?" I think that's how we cope with each other really.'

Also, being out at work may be somewhat acceptable. One teacher related to her experience at a staff party:

> 'I brought my lover to the party. We were pissed out of our minds. The others who weren't members of staff didn't know we were lesbians. I suppose you could say that they gradually found out. At first, everyone who didn't know was taking notice. But gradually as the party went on and more of us got pissed, we were no longer the centre of attention. In fact, we danced very close and were groping each other as the party went on. And no one noticed.'

The above 'I don't care' attitude seems peculiar to the out lesbian. She tends to have enough emotional security to accept the possibility of social disapproval or negativity. Perhaps, this is because the choice to come out is made. She appears to accept the social label 'lesbian'. Yet in reality she is re-creating with others a more positive stance in relationship to it. She discovers lesbianism as a way of life rather than a particular sexual orientation and she projects this revelation into all or most social activity. It becomes a total reality which colours all her activities as a woman in society.

'I guess I could say I'm a lesbian all of the time – 24 hours – even
when I eat, drink, sleep . . . . It's not some separate part of me. I'm
trying not to hide it any more. It's me as a woman.'

The out lesbian rejects society's image of 'deviant' or 'pseudo male'
by creating an alternative way of life for women in general and lesbians
in particular. As we saw earlier this alternative is imbued with choice.
However, this choice does not usually include the choice to be a man.
After talking with hundreds of lesbians throughout Great Britain, I
have met only two lesbians who wanted to be men. One lesbian, a
doctor and aged 45 said:

'I always wanted to be a man. I used to have dreams that I had a
penis and would make love to women. When I woke up I was so
disappointed because it wasn't true. In many ways, I think men
are so brutal yet I would have preferred to be one. It would have
been much easier for me as a doctor. You don't have a hard time of
it like I've had.'

The other lesbian, a writer and aged 29 said:

'I wished I were a man. After all they're the ones with the power and
run the world. Having a penis means power. It's true. If I were a man
provided I had the same intelligence I'd really go places.'

These two lesbians desired to be men. Yet, perhaps they wanted more
than a penis. They desired the social power that comes from being a man
in a male-orientated society, especially in their respective professions.

The lesbians in this study are categorized predominantly as out
lesbians in varying degrees. These lesbians view their identity as a threat
to this male-orientated society. As one lesbian states: 'It's not we who
are sick, fucked up or perverted. It's society that's fucked up.'

Lesbian relationships

You may wonder why lesbian relationships need any explanation or
why they merit discussion. However, lesbian relationships refer to the
varying types (with whom?, where? and why?) of relationships which
lesbians have by the very fact that they are lesbian-orientated. This

definition obviously challenges one's preconception of the lesbian as a 'purely sexual creature'. After all, a lesbian, like anyone else, is a social being. Furthermore, if given thought, the idea that her relationships are built upon meetings with others and develop from being a woman as well as a lesbian emerges. She may socialize with people or in places where others don't. But, in considering this fact and given the divisions within and complexities of modern social life, we experience similar situations within our own lives in relationship to the lives of other people. The difference, of course, is that our network of relationships, however complex they might be, do not extend to a 'deviant' sub-culture, or perhaps they do.

As lesbians come out of the closet, they form relationships generally within society at large and specifically within the lesbian ghetto (if these divisions are made). The lesbian ghetto refers to those pockets of lesbian social activity which are distributed throughout society. On the face of it, society sets up proscriptions – 'You shouldn't be a lesbian' – as well as prescriptions – 'If you are a lesbian, at least you should keep it hidden in those areas which have been demarcated for you – like the lesbian ghetto' – for the lesbian's social behaviour and determines her relationships within her particular social situation. In other words, lesbian relationships are framed within dual yet overlapping and conflicting social contexts – society and the ghetto. The ghetto is an immediate frame of reference because society continually attempts to isolate the lesbian within it. This does not imply that meaningful relationships cannot be found outside the ghetto, as indeed they are.

However, society's attempt to isolate or 'privatize' lesbianism does establish boundaries between 'unacceptable' social life and normality. Because a lesbian contravenes social norms, she is punished. Society's view is that she possesses a flaw or weakness as a social being. In a sense, she is banished from social recognition and from society's support. Yet, this banishment activates the creation of an 'alternative society', a sub-culture – the lesbian ghetto. Seemingly removed from the mainstream of social life, the ghetto is rooted in it and merely exposes oppression as 'endemic' to the established order. Its very existence not only challenges the establishment but also wears down its claim to legitimacy.

'I think that the last thousands of years we've been stopped off from relating to each other by a male-dominated civilization. I'm sure that that has freaked out or made lots of women feel really lonely over hundreds of years. I think that now just by the fact that I'm living with these other women who I love very much it's just a sign that things are going to change. Women are going to relate to women again like the way they used to in the old matriarchal times.'

Society attempts to subvert lesbian consciousness and to remove it from any form of group acceptability. Ironically, this subversion process effects a certain awareness through the development of the ghetto experience. Primarily through its 'ideology makers' society thinks, 'Lesbianism is probably inevitable. There will always be queers about. But let's cordon off this "dyke zone" from meaningful social life.' These views set up unnecessary conflicts and act as a divisive force for the emergence of lesbianism. None the less, with the expansion of the ghetto into a wide range of areas and activities this 'insulation effect' is thwarted. Furthermore, it appears that as more lesbians generate social organization and collective social action through the ghetto, they gain momentum as a potential threat to society. Their social effectiveness is measured by group visibility, deviant or otherwise. Therefore, the ghetto holds the key to their resistance to society and to their ultimate emergence as a social force. The establishment of meaningful lesbian relationships and the subsequent organization of these into a complex web of social reaction give the initial impetus for effective collective action through the ghetto.

In examining lesbian relationships, let us look at all these possibilities – where they might be established, what forms they might take, what types might appear and with whom they might be established.

The ghetto: where lesbians socialize

Lesbians tend to socialize in the 'bar scene', the 'club scene', the 'disco scene' and in what I term 'the ghetto within the ghetto'.

All these 'scenes' or settings have in common the spatial potential for forming lasting relationships with friends or lovers. All expose some lesbians' need for group support. Within the group, façades which have been built up over time in confrontation with society break down. How shy a lesbian may or may not be is not of primary importance. What is important is that, if somewhat closeted, she need not hide any longer in these contexts.

'I like being able to relax in a bar where I don't have to worry any longer if anyone is watching me and what I'm doing or stares at me.'

'Once a week I come along to —— [lesbian club] with friends just to get out of the rat race.'

The bar scene and the club scene provide an atmosphere which is somewhat relaxed and informal. These settings are usually characterized as totally lesbian-orientated, women-orientated (women only) or mixed gay (gay men and women) orientated. There is a variety of these types of places dispersed throughout major cities in Great Britain. Lesbians come to know about them through various media — gay (*Gay News*), lesbian (*Sappho*), women (*Newsletters*) or 'trendy' straight (*Time Out*) and through friends.

Bars create an environment in which drinking and chatting become the basis of socializing, while clubs usually include dancing as well. Clubs also require a membership fee which possibly involves more control of the actual number of participants than the bar scene.

Sometimes lesbians question the 'inflated value' of alcohol or their prices which appear to be much higher in these settings in comparison with straight bars and clubs.

'I guess if you're a lesbian and like to drink that's the price we have to pay. But, I don't like it and it doesn't make it right just because we are lesbians.'

'Lesbians and gays in general have always been oppressed by these bars — sometimes by the 'sex meat-market' which is a part of it but mostly by the outrageous prices of drinks. Still, we have to have some fun. That's how the system operates. If we have to have fun why not rip us off in the whole deal and make a profit off of our backs.'

The 'money factor' as well as the sexual (sexist 'meat-market') tone of clubs and bars may discourage otherwise sympathetic lesbians from participation.

During the past few years, some lesbians have actively boycotted establishments with these sorts of policies. They set up alternative places to socialize within their own areas. As a result, relationships are formed and maintained in neighbourhood locals as lesbians 'stake out' suitable 'lesbian hangouts'. Suitability is determined by the relative ease with which a lesbian is able to socialize in a 'non-oppressive environment'. Surprisingly, some local pubs may pass the suitability test.

'We go to —— [pub in area] and meet almost every night, a group of us . . . just for a few hours. We chat and see how we all are. All the people in the pub know us. They may think we're straight or maybe a strange lot of straights but whatever they don't let on.'

'I've been going to —— [local pub] ever since I've lived in this area . . . about 3 years now. I always bring my friends here and the barmaid knows . . . . She must know with all our arms around each other. But she has always been nice to me.'

In some areas, 'lesbian takeovers' of local pubs are evident. At times, lesbian participants may outweigh the straight ones. Sometimes, however, the effects of these takeovers spell disaster. If intimidation and abuse usually occurs for non-conforming groups in society, this becomes strikingly clear for lesbians.

It is particularly relevant to recall an incident in which a group of lesbians were attacked by a group of men. Both groups had been drinking at a local pub. However, the lesbians were in the majority. They suffered not only from verbal intimidation and abuse but also from physical attack. The results were that two of the lesbians involved were injured and sent to hospital and the police, who were investigating the case, would not press charges against the men.

'I was actually there. —— [a lesbian friend] was one who was beaten up along with ——. We were trying to get through to pull these men off. It was really weird because I've never seen that before. Something went in their heads. They realized with all these lesbians that they were redundant and it was a sexual frenzy. It really was. It was like some kind of orgasmic thing for them because they went bananas. The blood made them go bananas. There were about a half dozen of them. Something went off in their heads and they just couldn't handle it. Bif, bif, bif, because all of these women didn't need them in any single way at all. They could not handle it at all and one man said to one of the women, "Five minutes alone with me, dear, I'd show you what it is all about." I mean if I'd heard that once I've heard that a thousand million times from these stupid wanking men. Why can't they stick their stupid pricks up each other? I mean they would probably have a nicer time.'

Another lesbian recalling this incident said:

'Some women feel it's a male conspiracy. I don't feel this. I think it's just the patriarchy so ingrained in us, in everybody. In a male society being dominant for so long this is how they do it but I don't care whether it is conscious or unconscious. What happened at — when those men beat up the women is possibly a part of a conspiracy of silence. But they can't do it because we're all together in there and the trouble is we don't play them by their tactics. If we played it by their game they would beat us every time. But, we're doing it a different way and that means they can't touch us. I mean we might come to really heavy scenes. Who knows? But, they just don't understand our psyche and never have done. Thank God! that's why we're laughing in the end.'

The club and the bar scene appear to be orientated towards the creation of lesbians as an 'out group' or as a non-conforming group. Yet, in these contexts, one is made aware, through particular behaviour, dress, language and ambiance, that society is the 'out group'. Furthermore, any intrusion from an outsider or a non-lesbian is usually obvious to the participants and an embarrassing experience for the outsider. Outsiders, as in the case of the group that attacked the lesbians, may invade the ghetto through sheer brute force and this risk is always present for the lesbian. During the past few years in London, some lesbian clubs have also been the target of harassment from various groups. Also drug raids are not uncommon. In one incident in particular the raid was useless because no lesbians were found in possession of drugs. These examples illustrate the risk lesbians do take even when they socialize within their 'own' contexts.

With the development of the women's liberation movement, the idea of women coming together autonomously from men created women's discos. These discos upheld the notion of 'sisterhood' and provided an atmosphere characterized by singing and dancing. Organizers emphasize that discos are open to all women. They attempt to create a sense of the solidarity of women, a sense which is often lost at the usual straight disco.

'I went to this disco [straight disco] on Saturday night. I just
wanted to dance. I danced with some of the women there – my
lesbian friends and straight women that I knew. I was a bit
uncomfortable, I suppose because I wasn't pissed. I usually don't
care. In the end, I thought I just can't let it worry me because the
men around were just irrelevant and of course, this is what freaks
them out even more. If they're irrelevant, they can't stick their
big dick up you. It's strange how they tried to dance with some of
my straight friends [women] but they wanted to dance with each
other and us. But, it still was strange the whole thing.'

Similarly, a straight woman may feel out of place or uneasy at a women's
disco with a predominant lesbian population: 'I enjoyed it very much,
all these women dancing .... I wished more straight women were
there. I felt a little out of place as if I didn't really fit in.' This straight
woman was looking for support from other straight women. Since she
sensed this presence as a minority, she became a self-conscious parti-
cipant and was a marginal member of the disco, though it was for
women. As a result, she perceived the difference between defining
oneself as a lesbian and as a straight woman.

Within the past three years in London the number of women's
discos has increased from three to ten. This increase may reflect not
only the growing popularity they have for women's groups but also the
breaking down of barriers between lesbian and straight women within
the women's liberation movement. Perhaps straight women will no
longer be a minority group at these discos and as a result they will
become less self-conscious.

Some lesbians choose to live most or all of their social lives with
other lesbians. They create a 'ghetto within a ghetto' and tend to live
with friends, lovers, etc. in similar neighbourhoods. As a result they
develop close relationship networks which provide a unique, immediate
and continual support system. A case study of 'the ghetto within the
lesbian ghetto' will be presented in Chapter 6. A descriptive account of
the social implications of this type of ghetto will be discussed with
special reference to the lesbian feminist ghetto in London. However, for
our immediate purpose, we will focus on its effect upon relationship
networks.

These ghettos have a tendency to be spatially defined, while providing a complex system of social organization including a promotion system
which gives movement up the 'status hierarchy', a particular lesbian

ideology, group identity, language, life-style and dress. In reality, these ghettos represent sub-groupings within the total lesbian ghetto:

'I have recently moved to London and live in — [ghetto within ghetto] . After these past few weeks, I realized that there are certain ways of doing things and that these are very much a part of my new living arrangement. I had certain beliefs about myself which I feel are best expressed here. They are like the other women's. At first, I responded in these ways and became more accepted by the group. I felt as if I was being promoted by the others. I was growing up from a "baby lesbian" into a grown-up one.'

I have observed the growth of three such ghettos throughout the London area as well as others throughout Britain. A particular lesbian group which forms the base exerts subtle and sometimes great pressure upon an individual to conform to the specific dynamics of living within this system. And yet, the rewards are valued because individuals involved become 'bona fide' members as well as receive a large amount of group support and emotional security. As a result, a lesbian need nc venture outside her immediate 'reference group' to establish meaningful relationships. Furthermore, those who live outside this ghetto and who experience similar lesbian practice may not have daily contact with the ghetto or may not duplicate this experience. Nevertheless, these 'lesbian outsiders' may receive implicit support from the ghetto.

'I couldn't live there because of my work. I'd find it distracting. My work has priority right now. I uphold everything those women are doing. Our movement needs them. I do feel that I could go there any time day or night and someone would be there to listen or just have a good time.'

'I go there lots of times during the week for supper. They're all good friends. Once, I almost moved there.'

These 'lesbian outsiders' may either socialize in the ghetto, in parties, meals, visits, etc., or go with friends outside the ghettos to bars, clubs or discos. However, regardless of the reasons for her social distance from the ghetto, whether through lack of time, a pressing job, present living situation or lack of familiarity with it, the 'lesbian outsider' finds that her contact with it may imply a different type of relationship

network from one experienced by 'lesbian insiders'. As a partial partici-
pant, she develops alternative means of socializing as well as a different
perception of her 'home ground'. The existence of ghettos within the
ghetto demonstrates most clearly lesbianism as a total reality and
actively creates a new alternative for lesbians.

> Lesbianism is a way of living: with assumptions on the value and
> meaning of the self; it constitutes a kind of statement of belief of
> independence and freedom for all females. Society denies itself
> the opportunity to learn more about women and how they can
> function by making the Lesbian seal off her Lesbianism in all
> interactions with society.[2]

Perhaps, this explicit 'sealing off' as indicated by the above ghetto
may be the result of society's denial. However, if consciously undertaken, it may also become one of the ways in which this denial is
challenged.

Friends and lovers

The following discussion will examine the various types or forms which
appear and the specific content or dynamics of control which characterize lesbian relationships.

Initially, although not losing sight of the fact that some lesbians do
not make a clear-cut distinction between friends and lovers, I will discuss lover relationships. Next, I will look at how friendships are of
primary importance for a lesbian.

The types of 'lover' relationships

Simply, lovers include the person or persons with whom a lesbian is
currently having a sexual relationship. These types include: monogamy,
affairs, multiple relationships, primary relationships and secondary
relationships.

Monogamy is usually based upon the most common form of sexual
relationship in society. It upholds the ways in which heterosexuals
relate and is epitomized in the legal contract of marriage (albeit there
have been no lesbian marriages recorded in Great Britain). It is general

knowledge that heterosexuality is 'institutionalized' or structured in society through the marital bond of husband and wife and ultimately legitimated legally. Through this process the family emerges.

For the lesbian, monogamy becomes a relationship in which two individuals establish an exclusive and somewhat permanent bond. The relationship is usually explicitly sexual. Both parties attempt to preserve the primacy of the other partner in relationship to themselves.

Within the lesbian ghetto, monogamy may be criticized as an 'aping of heterosexual society':

'After all, marriage is a way in which men control women in an exclusive relationship. Why should we try to do the same and control each other in the same way?'

'I found increasingly the more I thought about it that this is exactly how a male system works. Men keep women isolated from each other for money or for their own bloody egos. And if one woman is prettier than the other, the other gets jealous. If only women can see what is being done to them.'

These critics are fearful because the potential for misuse of power, manipulation or control seemed almost inevitable in a monogamous situation.

In a different light, some view it as a viable form of relating because it provides one with a sense of security and energy direction:

'One of the reasons I like being with —— [lover's name] is that it's a cosy nest. I mean I find warmth in this sort of place. I feel people who dot about are very dangerous because they dot about all over the place. They don't have this sort of cosy warm, that's why I am sort of against it — I guess it's quite unreasoned. Yet, they don't have a home bit and I find this rather frightening . . . I like to build a nest and build a life where half is mine and half is somebody else's.'

'I have been with —— [lover's name] for a year. I am not totally convinced in the glories of monogamy because I know the problems with it. But, it's the easiest way for me right now.'

'I see —— [lover's name] as my security.'

The lesbian affair is similar to those which exist in heterosexual marriages and is a sexual relationship which challenges the notion of exclusivity for the monogamous partners. It tends to be a clandestine experience which is shared solely by the two involved. This choice may be either a 'fling' (a fleeting relationship after which exclusivity is restored) or the cause for a monogamous relationship to be transformed into a primary one. However, this transformation usually becomes gradually evident to the other 'excluded' monogamous partner, who is not immediately involved in the affair. Objectively, the affair may imply potential destruction of the ideals of monogamy and threaten the previously upheld notion of exclusivity. However, affairs may not have these effects, depending upon the degree of openness, friendship ties and emotional stability which emerge in this triangular experience.

Multiple relationships are grounded on the principle that a lesbian can have meaningful sexual relationships with more than one woman at any given time. For the individual, the rationale for establishing these relationships is twofold. First, she believes that she will learn much from giving and taking in reciprocity with others. Second, she feels one person should not become her ultimate emotional focus, or further, the sole source for the satisfaction of her sexual needs. For her, several women help to fulfill these emotional and sexual needs and vice versa. One relationship does not take priority over and above another in terms of one's total need fulfilment as a woman. Lesbians in the above relationships have varying feelings:

'I think what I like is the very openness of them. I mean straight women have nice chats with their friends. But, I still don't think it's anything like the relating some of us do. I mean I can't speak for all lesbians, I mean I speak for me and the people I know. I mean women can't be like that because they are ashamed of what you can't talk about or there are feeling which you can't express.'

'Even after sexual relationships with them, they have developed into close friendships.'

'I can't see how a sexual expression of something emotional can be seen as unnatural or odd.'

'I don't think of myself as radical because of these relationships. Because the thing is I got so used to thinking the way I do that I no longer see it as radical. Sometimes, in straight company I'm termed as extremist because of the way I live my life and how I relate. I don't see myself as such. I just care for lots of women in lots of ways. It's perfectly natural for me to think this way now.'

Vulnerability and personal struggle as well as support may result. However, these relationships may be difficult to cope with for some:

'I mean there are certain circumstances which made me feel particularly vulnerable . . . . It's very important to put yourself in the other woman's position and see what the situation is . . . not to see everything in terms of your own ego . . . but, I'm a very egotistical person and I find it difficult.'

'The women I live with are much older and have had these feeling for a much longer time. I've felt slightly as if I've been hanging behind and I've never felt on equal footing in a way. I feel insecure, I suppose I mean they don't put shit on me it's all my own feelings of inadequacy which again is born of a heterosexual way of relating. . . . It's so vile all the conditioning. It's difficult to handle no matter how much support you get from the others.'

And it may be especially difficult for those who are new to this way of relating:

'I know very soon I'll feel it in my head. It's just a question of time. The point about being new to it is that you've got to make things up on our way. We've got to learn new ways of doing things. We have no guidelines and we're fumbling about. All we've got to go on is our love for each other and our attempts at honesty. We make lots of mistakes and there is lots of pain.'

Interestingly enough some lesbians espouse multiple relationships as an ideal (along with the desired effects of equality between women), while implicitly or explicitly establishing a primary relationship with one partner. Thus, the theory is upheld, while the practice is not. This demonstrates the perennial tension created between a lesbian's personal life and political life.

The group rationale for maintaining these 'non-exclusive', caring relationships is that 'exclusivity is anti-women'. Specific lesbian ideologies lend support to the idea that the powerlessness of women is perpetuated by isolation, exclusivity and over-possessiveness — all of which, in the end, are solidified in heterosexual marriage. In these contexts, men hold the reins of power. Therefore, lesbians not only define them as anti-women, male-orientated, etc. but also scorn any social relationship in which the need for control, power, possessiveness, etc. take priority over the desire for human communication through love, caring and sensitivity. For them the power of women emerges by the breaking down of traditional sexual barriers and hierarchies between women, between men and women or both (for some):

> 'I think of these straight women. Some of them are not real people because they are not allowed to be. If they are strong and relating to men, they're just half-people, even if they do talk to you. You know it's all what some men have told them anyway. Because they have been oppressed so much, they feel as if they wouldn't know anyway. They couldn't handle it. Whereas in our scene, it's just that you never feel ashamed or that someone is going to put you down or even mock you. We talk about things. Whereas in a straight society things like this never come to the surface. Women never really have a chance.'

> 'I'd like everyone to be liberated. I'm a bit liberal. I feel that I'm beginning to come around to the theory that through my experiences with women the only way is through women. I know if women get themselves together, men can do what they like. No one is going to have anything to do with them. So they can do what they like and have a lovely time and blow each other up. You know Henry Kissinger could have brought about the end of this male-dominated society?

From an observational viewpoint, a great amount of mobility, time, effort, emotional energy, flexibility and personal security is required. These factors make it difficult to sustain multiple relationships over long periods of time. Often this lesbian practice is challenged, when 'falling in love' occurs. Lesbians are then faced with the dilemma of living out the romantic love ideal, while denying its validity. This contradiction exposes the power of the dominant ideology and its effect upon one's sexual life and, in this case, one's political practice.

Primary relationships imply the notion, as in monogamy, of putting another woman first. However, unlike monogamy, they uphold the belief in a non-exclusive sexual relationship. A lesbian has a caring friendship with a woman (who is viewed as primary). Yet, the option to relate to others is open. If one partner or both partners act out this option, they establish secondary relationships:

> 'I'm having another scene with another woman. —— [lover in primary relationship] finds it difficult. The fact is that it is completely above board and everything is talked about. Whatever she wants to ask me – for example what we do in bed, she gets told. You begin to realize the way you do relate. I suppose it starts off relating to a lover and then you have close friends and you can talk about anything to them. You get confidence within yourself and you can get it with other people.'

The primacy of the initial relationship may not be retained, as I soon discovered had occurred with the above lesbian. Furthermore, the experience of relating to a secondary partner becomes more worthwhile and becomes transformed into a new primary relationship. As an operating principle, non-exclusive love may activate this risk. However, if this principle goes by the wayside, primary relationships develop into monogamous ones. As a result, outside relationships are perceived by both partners as threatening and potential affairs. Perhaps these problems emerge from the process of separating real love, which is viewed as non-exclusive for these lesbians, from the notion of primary relationships, in which exclusive love is an integral part for 'straight society' and which implies relating to only one partner.

It is interesting to note how these dynamics affect the 'other party' or 'non-participant' in the primary relationship. She may view herself or be viewed by the others as powerless, defenceless or expendable. This secondary status or experience of being an outsider may correspond to the frustrations, emotional instability and insecurity which arise in the affair.

> 'I felt hurt by the whole thing, knowing that —— would ultimately go back to ——. Yet, I couldn't stop caring for her.'

> 'For a few months, I got involved in a series of relationships one right after the other where I was the third party. It was good – no pressure, no real dependence, no deep involvement, just friendship

and caring. But after it all, I knew I was the last one on the list and I wanted someone to care for me in a special way.'

The content of lover relationships

More often than not sexual relationships bring with them the use of power whether in the form of brute force, as in rape, economic control, as in marriage, or sexual hierarchies, as with male dominance and female subservience. All indicate sexism. Lesbian relationships are not free from power and one may find any of the above forms within them: 'Lesbians can be just as sexist as men, so can women be for that matter.'

The following discussion will be concerned with the last aspect of the use of power: sexual hierarchies in sexual politics. It may be a model for structuring lesbian lover relationships. Three structures are evident and demonstrate the content of lesbian relationships. They are the traditional butch and femme relationship, in which power is overt, the dominant and submissive relationship, in which power is subtle, and equal relationships, in which power is minimal.

The use of power and control to maintain a relationship is overt when lesbians live out the traditional stereotypes of the butch and the femme which society has presented for them to appropriate. These stereotypes are dependent upon the control of the femme − the passive, dependent, secondary, female-orientated partner − by the butch − the dominant, independent, primary, aggressive, male-orientated partner. A situation of inequality or inferiority for the femme is created. Both partners respond to each other in a way similar to the straight heterosexual couple. Ironically, as lesbians, they act out 'straight' sex roles or ape a straight society. They are usually referred to as 'straight lesbians' by other lesbians.

I have observed some lesbians who do form these relationships. However, surprisingly to some, they were in a very small minority. Most lesbians I observed had relationships in which the interplay of power remained subtle. Although situations of control and manipulation are evident, power is not easily recognized as in the butch-femme relationship. A dominant role, held by the partner who controls the relationship as well as a submissive role, held by the partner who acquiesces, may be held for the entire span of the relationship, for most of the relationship or for some of the relationship.

The distinguishing characteristic is that at a certain point in time due to a variety of factors (lesbian ideology, living situation, physical health, and so on) one partner is dominant or has more control in the relationship. Yet, at another time, the opposite may be true. In other words, the roles are reversible or interchangeable. Power does intrude as a subtle force, but does not remain the principal *modus operandi* as in the butch and femme relationship. I would contend that this way of relating is important because it represents a transitional stage in the development of lesbian consciousness and the movement away from traditional social stereotypes.

'When I first had these scenes with this woman, ——, which seems like a long time ago, I kind of knew that I was a lesbian, but I couldn't bring myself to it, or to say it. I am a very out-doors person, very handy around the house. I mean I used to do all these sorts of things for my mother. When I met —— she was a kind of femme dolly-bird type. But she changed and I did too. I guess it was a certain amount of role playing. I even think that it wasn't as heavy as the really butch and femme types. We really weren't on that trip. Anyways I never understood that sort of thing. I didn't realize how we were living that we were oppressed or how I didn't relate it to the sort of oppression of blacks, Jews, women whatever.'

The quest for equality is a desire for the minimal use of power, ultimately powerlessness, or vulnerability in one's intimate relationships. The latter idea, vulnerability, emerged from the theory of the women's liberation movement and was first developed by Shulamith Firestone:

Love is the height of selfishness; the self attempts to enrich itself through the absorption of another. Love is being psychically wide-open to another. It is a situation of total emotional vulnerability. Therefore, it must be not only the incorporation of the other, but an exchange of selves. Anything short of this exchange will hurt one or the other party.[3]

The practice of equality is rooted in the rise of lesbian consciousness. In the ghetto, it exists in seed form. Apart from the fact that I had to uncover areas in the ghetto where this stage of awareness was possible I found it not only difficult to observe, but an infrequent occurrence.

As barely visible, this relationship involves discreet interaction between two women who attempt to break down 'power plays', 'manipulation' or 'game playing'. Honesty, trust and openness become the order of the day. Lesbians rely upon their own emotional vulnerability and powerlessness and attempt to create situations of caring. Commitment to the 'other' or others are made, but the primary commitment is to oneself as a woman. Here autonomy, not dependence, in the field of human relationships is the key. Thus, they believe that independence and assertiveness combined with vulnerability and trust minimize power: 'I always think of this question: "Are you willing to share your autonomous self and sexuality with me?'

Some lesbians believe that equality is possible only in and through relationships with women. They believe that relationships between men and women will never be equal until society has a radical change on the level of structure (patriarchy, capitalism or both). However, because they tend to over-emphasize patriarchy and more specifically, male power, they are not aware of or deny the importance of capitalism as another power source. For them, on the level of human relationships, the intrusion of power is predominantly 'male'. Yet, in reality, this intrusion is dominance-orientated, whether sexual, economic, physical, racial, or whatever, in society. As a result full consciousness is obstructed. Difficulties arise when they attempt to justify not only relating to men but establishing equality with them. Only relationships between women have the potential to be equal:

'It's easier for me to relate to women because we're equal full stop.'

'Because society is the way it is and women are oppressed. I could never have an equal relationship with any man. So I decided to become a lesbian. I suppose some people in society as well as women in the movement are critical of me, but it's the only way for me.'

'I never really related to men. I slept with them. I never enjoyed it, because of the way they treated me like some receptacle. Most of my male friends are queer, but it's not that I hate men I mean I hate what a male society has done to me and millions of women. With a woman I feel myself and equal.'

The importance of friendships

The old adage, 'No man is an island' (we should add 'or woman') applies to lesbians as well. Like most people, they rely upon friends as a source of emotional growth. For oppressed people in society, friendships are particularly important. It is through them that one's experience of oppression becomes a gift to another. A burden is lifted. Personhood is shared. Consciousness is raised. Views are exchanged. Isolation is broken down. Perhaps, an insight into the struggle of another is gained. And, if only in a very minimal way, society moves forward.

Some lesbians seek friends who are sympathetic to or understanding of their struggle. However, for others this is not the case and they remain isolated, fearful, hidden and unhappy.

Many lesbians find a unique friendship network with other lesbians who themselves share the same oppression. There is a large pool from which a lesbian's friends are drawn — schoolmates, workmates, housemates, neighbours, relatives, present lovers (for those who don't make a distinction between friends and lovers), and former lovers. For an individual, a cohesive network of friendships may be formed. It is with her lesbian friends that not only the existence of oppression but also the experience of it is most deeply felt. Lesbian liberation becomes, if only for a fleeting moment, a shared, heartfelt encounter and therefore a real possibility. As bonds of solidarity between lesbian friends are established, lesbian practice emerges. It is, perhaps, within such bonds that a sense of urgency is most keenly perceived and hopes are raised for the future. The tools for coping with the struggle are fashioned in mind, heart and hand.

Often a lesbian forms close friendship ties with women who are non-lesbians, either straight or bi-sexual, and who may or may not be aware of her lesbianism. This latter awareness depends upon trust and openness on the part of the lesbian. On the one hand, openness may imply the risk of losing a friend, and 'gaining an enemy', as some lesbians say. On the other hand, it may lead to close ties which are based upon women's experience. However, sometimes disclosure is difficult:

'I am afraid to tell —— [straight friend] because she may not want to be my friend anymore. I know that she likes me, but maybe she'll feel I'll pounce on her which of course doesn't even enter into the picture.'

One lesbian expressed frustration when she found it almost impossible to be open with her friend. She valued their friendship, which went back to childhood days, yet she asked: 'How can — be a true friend, if she doesn't know I'm a lesbian? But, I'm so afraid if she does find out, she won't be my friend.' For this lesbian, her lesbianism was an integral part of her life. However, when she had problems in her relationship with her lover and when the relationship finally ended, she was unable to communicate openly her feelings with this friend. Yet, when her friend had similar problems with male lovers, she felt free to discuss them with her 'unknown' lesbian friend.

Many lesbians do have men friends, whatever society may choose to believe to the contrary. Unlike society's images of the 'man-hater', 'castrating bitch' or 'Amazonian warrior', lesbians establish warm relationships with some men, who can be gay or straight.

If a man is gay, he shares homosexual oppression with a lesbian and is therefore potentially aware of the lesbian experience. They may socialize together in pubs, bars and clubs and form close bonds. Because of the absence of the sexual element, which usually characterizes a close relationship between a straight man and a straight women, they feel at ease. However, if a gay man uses his 'social superiority' as a man to oppress a lesbian, he may risk losing a friend. Regardless of a shared oppression, the gay man takes a gamble if he is sexist towards her. The more a lesbian is conscious of the oppressive features of a patriarchal society and those who use these features against her, the more she will spurn relationships with those who incorporate anti-women feelings within theirs. A gay man may be included within this field and therefore, excluded from hers:

'I like gay men, if they are feminists. If they are not, they drive me insane because of their behaviour which is conditioning they perpetuate. They really get into it and work on it, to get all these mannerisms.'

Some lesbians who regularly relate to gay men expressed mixed feelings:

'It really is an individual thing. I have found that some gay men are as oppressive as straight men. But, in general they are the only category of men who have a chance to be non-sexist towards women or any hope of serving in a feminist society.'

'I don't know just about any men. We do have certain friends. They
are — and — [gay men friends] . I never think of them as being
men. Well, when I think of when most men want friendship, they
always tell you, especially when they get drunk, this happened to
me anyways, that they want to screw you. I mean these fellows
[gay men friends] I know when I see them and when they are with
us they are just who they are. But, I don't see them with any other
women. So, I don't know how they treat them. They are probably
more aware. But, I'm sure that they can slip back into being male
chauvinist pigs like anyone else I know.'

Another lesbian who didn't have any gay men friends expressed her
attitudes towards them as a group:

'I know of all the sorts. I meet some and they seem to be
exaggerated queens and I must say I don't see why or I don't think
that a gay man needs to be effeminate or feminine. I don't see why
he has to sort of put on make-up or do those sorts of things. I know
I'm sounding narrow-minded. I haven't met many straight type of
gay men or ones I mean who are like the average people you met. I
always come across the very exaggerated types or those who attempt
to be vicious or have all the bad qualities of a woman as opposed to
the good ones. But, I really don't know enough of them really.'

Other lesbians who did have close friends who were gay men had
positive feelings towards them:

'I like gay men very much. Yes, very much.'

'I like gay men. I just don't like theatrical gays or the queens or role-
playing ones, but the everyday gay, I like very much.'

'I like lots of gay men I meet. They are so easy to get on with
because there is no tension. My friends are kind, generous and
giving. Of course, the gay scene for a man is totally different than
it is for women. It's very much like the heterosexual scene with
lots of role-playing. I find it difficult to understand in terms of
how I feel. But when I think of — and — or — [gay men friends]
in comparison with straight men they are infinitely better in their
response to women. I think they're terrific.'

Lesbians have close relationships with straight men as well. How-ever, for some, if sexism rears its ugly head bonds of friendship may be broken. Generally, a straight man friend may appear as sympathetic or non-oppressive to her as a woman:

'I met — [straight man friend] last year. As far as I'm concerned he is a loving caring friend. After I came out, I was very much like a separatist. I hated men. Then I knew I couldn't do what I wanted if I didn't relate to men at all. I know I'm attractive as a woman and have always had difficulties with men because of this. But with — I feel that I think he's great and I love him just as deeply as I do any woman friend. I relate to him on a level that I never related to a man before. I don't know why. He has certainly become aware more of the problems of women since we've been friends.'

For some, the fear of a 'sexual come-on' may predominate in rela-tionships with straight men:

'Potentially, I could have as many straight men friends as I do straight women friends. I put up barriers because I know if I'm friendly with a man, he thinks, "God she's trying to get off with me." It's not my aim at all. So I put up barriers and I'm not as friendly to men as I could be.'

'I find it difficult to respond to men as friends – very, very difficult. I tend to ignore them. It's an effort to get to know a man. Whereas with women, it's not. With women, it's an instant thing. It's easy.'

Others exclude men altogether from their field of relationships. These lesbians call themselves 'separatists' because they separate themselves or cut themselves off from relating to any man:

'Keep them out of my way.'

'I don't have the energy or the time to relate to them. I don't even have the desire.'

'I just ignore them most of the time.'

Although separatists are in a minority in the lesbian population, they do tend to have extreme negative reactions to men:

'I fucking hate them.'

'Let them all go to hell in a row boat.'

Still other lesbians who are more closeted keep their lesbianism hidden and make it possible to 'play their games' (straight men's) as some call it:

'I know some men say I'm beautiful and why don't I get it off with them. I won't but I like the admiration of it all. I just tell them to get on with it, but not with me and they don't know why.'

One lesbian said that after she had defined herself as a lesbian, she experienced more confidence in her relationships with men:

'Before I came out, I was generally hostile towards men. I always felt they were the sexual aggressors. When I came out, my hostility was lowered. I found that I could have meaningful relationships with men. I plug into them intellectually. I feel relaxed because I know they no longer control me.'

This chapter has discussed generally the social reality of lesbianism and has given priority to the individual – her identity and her social relationships. The next chapter will examine the lesbian experience in light of the emergence of social lesbianism. The emphasis will be upon the development of group awareness and group identity for contemporary lesbians. This development manifests itself as a potential social force. Since this study is primarily about social lesbians, those with a group identity, the following chapter should serve as an entry into the major part of the work.

3 Social lesbians and social lesbianism: Who are they? What is 'it'?

The major contention of this book is that lesbianism is a changing social phenomenon. Social lesbianism or the development of a group identity as lesbians becomes the key to understanding how this change is occurring. This chapter will briefly look at three historical views of lesbianism. Then we will examine the social implications of one of these views, social lesbianism.

Three views of lesbianism

If we examine the emergence of lesbianism, we are able to trace historically three stages of development from the traditionalist view, the social view and the ideological view. These views have effects upon the formation of lesbian consciousness. Their development is neither smooth nor obvious and is often contradictory. An understanding of this process warrants the removal of the historical layers which have obscured our vision.

For their 'first' lesbian image interested observers looked to the followers of Queen Hatshepsut who is depicted throughout ancient Egypt in male costume and false beards; the Greek Amazon warriors who engaged in battle with their male counterparts in Asia Minor; Sappho's band of young women who lived on the island of Lesbos; the Roman women who during the feast of Saturnalia engaged in lesbian practices in honor of Bona Dea, or the holy virgins who inhabited the cloisters of medieval nunneries. When discovering what to them was the 'lesbian prototype', these observers tended to uphold the vision of a matriarchal order from which their image emerged. Regardless of these claims, society has been patriarchal for many years and within it lesbianism became an isolated social fact. Corresponding to this fact, lesbians were isolated social beings, having neither the awareness nor the group support to understand themselves and, furthermore, to merit social understanding. In whatever ways ideas about lesbianism and lesbians' ideas developed, these were dependent upon patriarchal society's view of women during a particular historical period.

The seeds of lesbian awareness grew within seclusion, both conceptual and spatial. Thomas Szasz alludes to the transformation of the concept 'homosexual' from a religious and moral into a social and medical one. Yet, it is important to note that historically homosexuality is forbidden only for men:

> You shall not lie with a man as with a woman . . . God addresses males only. He does not command women not to lie with a female as with a man. Here, by omission and implication and elsewhere by more explicit phrasing, woman is treated as a kind of human animal, not as a full human being. The most up to date legal statutes of Western nations dealing with homosexuality continue to maintain this posture towards women: though homosexual intercourse between consenting adults continues to be prohibited in many countries nowhere does it apply to women.[1]

Within the context of British history, lesbianism has not been illegal.[2] In 1885 after the passage of the Criminal Law Amendment Bill (which made homosexual acts between adults punishable by law), Queen Victoria refused to sign the Bill unless all references to women were deleted (Delete Lesbianism!). Lesbianism was unthinkable to the Queen (Criminalize 'queens' only!). Therefore, lesbianism was written out of the law, but not out of existence.

Interestingly enough, in 1921 the attempt to introduce a new Criminal Amendment Bill which penalized 'acts of indecency by females' was unsuccessful. In a more contemporary light, the Sexual Offences Act of 1967 decriminalized homosexual acts which were carried out in private by adults, meaning men, over 21. In this case, women were again excluded from the legal domain and, furthermore, removed from the category 'adult'. Not only was lesbianism viewed as non-existent and therefore non-threatening, but also women were categorized as non-adults and therefore incapable of making 'a deviant choice' in a society ruled by men. Indeed, how could they?

The traditionalist view

In light of the above discussion, the initial view and stage of lesbian awareness was embedded in tradition. In this context, a lesbian, isolated and secluded from society, remains in the closet and is hidden from public view. Aware of her 'sickness', she is denied social recognition. Ideology makers, such as social workers, doctors and psychiatrists, who prescribe treatment and who may express 'curative' concerns deal with her on an individual level. She is in need of help. Society must take responsibility for its unfortunates who are born deformed or genetically inferior *or* who are socially abnormal or 'deviant'. 'It' (lesbianism) is a personal problem or disease which is characteristic of a genetic quirk, a psychological malfunctioning, a mental illness, immaturity, individual abnormality or, simply, a perversion. Analysts use terms like 'arrested heterosexuality', 'dominant mother', 'dominant father', 'abnormal hormones' or 'faulty genes' — all of which either caused the 'disease' and 'problem' or at least helped 'it' along.

Lesbianism becomes an individual thing and understanding it merits scientific observation similar to studying the effects from a rare, isolated bacteria strain in a pathology laboratory. When the cause of lesbianism is discovered, 'it' is treated accordingly. While some are hopeful that a cure is on the way, others prescribe the 'correct antidote' whether in the form of pills, a penis, patronizing or parental support. Lesbians who are bound up within this treatment process experience guilt, fear, frustration or misery. 'Sick lesbians' appear to suffer most from their affliction as well as from society's image of them. In effect, they are prevented from achieving lesbian consciousness. If consciousness exists, it may be subverted. Not only do they tend to accept a negative self-identity and a 'deviant' or unacceptable social label but they perpetuate these images of lesbianism throughout society. Unknowingly, they collude with this subversion process.

The social view

During the first part of this century, after the initial wave of feminism through the suffragette movement, it became apparent that lesbians organized socially as lesbians and in group settings such as bars and clubs. Becoming more visible, lesbianism was thrust into the public sphere of society. Whether or not lesbians consciously questioned traditional images of themselves, they manifested themselves, if only in a partial manner, in and through group contexts. Within these settings, a group identity emerged as it emerges today. A lesbian comes to the awareness that not only do other women like herself exist but also there are special places in which she can 'be herself'. Extreme isolation is broken down and if only for a brief moment, one is able to step out from behind the closet door. With the rise of social interaction amongst lesbians, society becomes increasingly more unable to individualize or personalize the phenomenon. Individual treatment is transformed into a supposed social understanding. Lesbianism is 'upgraded' to the status of a social problem. Implicitly, it achieves social recognition. Yet, in reality, this recognition is achieved only within 'socially designated areas' — the sub-culture of deviance. Any attempt to break down the barriers between the sub-culture of deviance and the dominant culture are thwarted. Thus lesbianism is again secluded from society, but this time on a larger scale. Liberals may even say, 'Lesbianism is not a social problem, but a social fact. What one does in bed is one's own affair.' From this, we see how the dominant culture, in its attempt to make divisions between sexuality and society as well as between lesbians and women, ultimately wins out. Consistent with tradition, lesbianism is privatized. Group development, albeit increasing, is subverted.

The ideological view

In recent years, lesbianism has been viewed within an ideological context and as a social force. With the emergence of the Gay Liberation Front (GLF) and the Women's Liberation Movement (WLM), new images of lesbianism have been presented to society. These images challenge both the traditional view and the social view. They develop from the idea that lesbian consciousness necessitates a particular form of lesbian practice — politics — as well as group awareness. In other words, lesbians are dared not only to 'come out of the closet' but to 'go out into the streets'. The emphasis is upon the emergence of lesbianism as a force to be reckoned with. It is only through struggle against oppression that this emergence becomes visible. Awareness becomes linked with women's total struggle within an oppressive social order. In this way, lesbianism becomes a social threat. And if society perceives this threat it attempts to annihilate it. (In Chapter 6, the effects of this process will be discussed in more detail.)

Lesbianism today

Briefly, we have looked at three views of lesbianism. They have historical roots within society. I would contend that they also have had an
impact upon lesbian consciousness and that they determine an individual lesbian's image of herself as being tradition-orientated, social-
orientated, or ideology-orientated. Furthermore, they reflect her lesbian
consciousness as being apolitical, pre-political or political, respectively.

It is important to remember that these three views of lesbianism
and the stages of consciousness are ever-present in society. We should
imagine a threefold spectrum which represents the lesbian phenomenon.
On it, there appears to be a temporal development from one view to
another as well as from one stage of awareness to another. However,
as with many elements of social life, the vestiges of the past survive in
the midst of hopes for the future. Therefore, we are able to distinguish
between the stages and views of lesbianism as well as to trace all three
existing in contemporary society. My major concern will not be to
isolate these elements. To isolate would be typical of analyses of
lesbians and would collude with tradition. Rather, I will attempt to
draw a total and clear picture of the lesbian situation as it exists today.

This study is about social lesbians – those who develop within the
second or 'social' view and who have reached a pre-political stage of
awareness as a social group. However, this emphasis does not deny the
existence of the other views (traditional and ideological) or other stages
of awareness (apolitical and political). It merely exposes a transition
in the experience of lesbianism.

Whether we are aware of it or not, contemporary society is riddled
with all kinds of conflict and contradiction. Therefore, it is not surprising that within society, lesbianism also presents contradictory forces.
'Sick lesbians' who uphold traditional views exist, while lesbian feminists
espouse ideological ones. None the less, social lesbians offset this
polarity, but by no means do they reduce it nor mediate the social
conflict amongst lesbians and between lesbians and society. In fact,
they escalate opposition on both levels. As a distinct social grouping,
they make contradictions even more visible.

Emerging from a somewhat 'liberal society', social lesbians as a
'middle group', between traditional and ideological lesbians, expose
traces of both a traditionalist mentality and an ideological one. In
other words, they maintain elements of the past or of a previous
generation while pre-disposing themselves to a social force which

emerges from a political context. They embrace a conflicting, and furthermore contradictory, group identity.

On the one hand, social lesbianism establishes an identity which accepts the sickness of the individual, but which rejects remorse ('sick, but not sorry'). On the other hand, social lesbianism despises the sickness label and negates it totally. This latter negation ('sorry, but not sick') lends support to the ideological view and challenges tradition.

Both types together form social lesbianism, demonstrate the transformation of the lesbian experience, and imply a certain level of group consciousness as well as social responsiveness. It is through this prepolitical stage of awareness that lesbianism accumulates the potential to become a social force, a direct challenge to society.

The implications of social lesbianism

Chapter 4 will describe in detail both forms of social lesbianism as well as their respective social emergence. The immediate concern will be to locate the general area and to examine its social relevance for today's society. It will be necessary to build up a perspective in terms of the group's awareness and actual view of itself. Also, analysis will be directed towards how this group creates a social problem.

I stated previously that social lesbianism affords a more open lifestyle than the traditional one. It appears that more lesbians are 'out' than ever before.

In the questionnaire survey for this study (See Appendix 3) more than half (58 per cent) responded that they were 'out' to most of the people with whom they associated (see Table 3.1). Thirty-seven per cent responded that they were 'out' to their family, while 27 per cent related this to their workmates or schoolmates.

Furthermore, we see that in terms of the levels of 'outness' and 'closetedness' more lesbians had a tendency to be out (86 per cent) than not (13.5 per cent) (Table 3.2).

Table 3.2 presents us with a general picture of the varying degrees of outness and closetedness that social lesbians experience. The eight-point graduated scale was set up in order to generalize from Table 3.1 which relates to people in general, at work or college or in the family. The scale illustrates how social lesbians answered those questions. If a lesbian responded that most people in general, at work and in her family knew her to be a lesbian, she scored 111 on the answer and was

Table 3.1   *'The out life' and social lesbians*

QUESTION: 'Of those with whom you associate how many are
you "out" to?'

People in general	No.	%	Work or college	No.	%	Family	No.	%
Most	117	58.2	Most	55	27.4	Most	75	37.3
Some	56	27.9	Some	63	31.3	Some	31	15.4
Very few	20	10.0	Very few	40	19.9	Very few	37	18.4
None	7	3.5	None	42	20.9	None	58	29.9
NA	1	0.5	NA	1	0.5	NA	00	0.0
Total	201	100.0		201	100.0		201	100.0

NA = No Answer

Table 3.2   *The levels of 'outness' and 'closetedness'*

		No.	%	
Out	1	92	45.8	
	2	24	11.9	Tendency to be out = 173 = 86%
	3	25	12.4	
	4	32	15.9	
Closet	5	1	0.5	
	6	19	9.5	Tendency to be in the closet = 27 =
	7	–	–	13.5%
	8	7	3.5	NA = 1

categorized on Level 1 (Out) on the scale. If a lesbian responded that
none of the above knew, she scored 444 and was placed in Level 8.
Sixty-four possible scores were coded according to a lesbian's answer to
the questions. As a result, there were eight possible scores which related
to *each* of the eight levels on the scale.

What do these findings reveal? In an immediate sense, group contact
may imply openness and growth. We know that group identity develops
with individual awareness and vice versa.[3] If a lesbian 'plugs into' a
group context with a distinct identity, she finds support from others.
Along with this, a certain amount of lesbian knowledge is acquired. As
the process unfolds, lesbians attempt to justify their way of life. Within
this setting, lesbians create the necessary 'communicative tools' and
communication networks to build up these justifications. This process

aids an individual in explaining her social situation to 'outsiders', if the opportunity arises and/or if the desire to do so is present. Possibly, if these 'outsiders' are ignorant of what lesbianism entails, they are fed relevant information which originates from 'inside' the 'lesbian ghetto' or 'sub-cultural' experience. Although non-members, they become knowledgeable. Of course, this process is dependent upon the outness of social lesbians as well as their degree of contact with 'outsiders'.

'Two years ago I never could explain even to myself why I was a lesbian. Now I am able to talk about it. I told my sister last year and family friends recently. I can explain it easily now.'

'Well, you're able to come more to terms with yourself and willing to present yourself in terms of how you are and take what you need from others and not give out signals of being unsure or uncertain.'

These lesbians describe the effects of the group experience. With it, they become readily able to explain their way of life. The development of a group identity makes it easier to come out as well as to establish individual confidence. A lesbian knows she is not alone and this creates implicit, and sometimes explicit, support which carries her along.

The 'women before lesbian' factor

This study has consistently found that social lesbians tend to place themselves consciously or unconsciously within a feminist framework, somewhat related to their experience as women in society:

'I don't have a lesbian identity as such. I have an identity with women in general.'

'I have the sense of myself as a woman.'

'My life is not really different in terms of how feelings would be for other women. Obviously, for society there seems to be no commitment in terms of a paper binding you. In a way, it's a deeper commitment to women.'

'Absolutely all my energies are concerned with women.'

'We establish an identity with all women. It involves straight women and also doesn't exclude men.'

'I am a woman first, then a lesbian.'

From the above, we see that lesbians do not differentiate their feelings from those of other women. We sense that 'lesbian feelings' not only appear within the perspective of women in general but also emerge from those who have deep awarenesses as women in society.

Whether they view themselves in a predominantly sexual (having a sexual preference for women) or social (aware of strong ties with women) way, 75 per cent saw themselves primarily as women-identified (see Table 3.3).

Table 3.3   *The lesbian identity and women's identity*

QUESTION: 'Do you see your lesbian identity as being very much a part of or closely linked up with your identity as a woman?'

	No.	%
Yes	151	75.1
No	47	23.4
N.A.	3	1.5
Total	201	100.0

Furthermore, 83 per cent perceived that they were either totally or primarily committed to women in a male-orientated society (which appears to militate against this idea) (see Table 3.4).

When asked to define the relationship between lesbianism and feminism, 93 per cent established a relationship whether it was vague (48 per cent of 93 per cent) or close (52 per cent of 93 per cent). While 44 per cent of the total sample established a vague relationship between the two, 49 per cent expressed that both were closely linked or insepar-able. Although no one felt that one contradicted the other, 6 per cent did not relate the two. (See Table 3.5).

It is interesting to note that while social lesbianism illustrates a high level of 'women commitment' (83 per cent) and a close or primary identification with women (75 per cent), it does not (in terms of the majority) establish a *close* relationship between lesbianism and feminism.

Table 3.4   *The 'women commitment' vis à vis lesbianism*
QUESTION: 'How do you see yourself . . .'

	No.	%
(a) 'as a woman who is totally committed to women and seeks their company for social, emotional, psychological and sexual support?'	(a) 114 (totally or primarily 8% committed to women)	56.6
(b) 'as a woman who is primarily attracted to women for emotional, social and psychological support and who sometimes seeks the company of men for the satisfaction of these needs?'	(b) 55	27.4
(c) 'as a woman who is equally attracted to both men and women and who seeks emotional, sexual and psychological support from men and women equally.'	(c) 12	6.0
(d) Other	(d) 18	9.0
(e) NA	(e) 2	1.0
Total	201	100.0

Table 3.5   *Lesbianism and feminism*
QUESTION: 'Lesbianism and feminism . . .'

	No.	%	
(a) are contradictory	—	—	
(b) are closely related or inseparable	98	48.8	93%established some relationship
(c) are somewhat related	89	44.3	
(d) do not relate	13	6.5	6.5% did not relate lesbianism and feminism
(e) NA	1	0.5	

Table 3.6   *Lesbianism and the women's movement – as a key issue?*
QUESTION: 'Should lesbianism be one of the key issues in the women's movement?'

	No.	%
Yes	131	65.2
No	63	31.3
NA	7	3.5
Total	201	100.0

(Less than half, 49 per cent, established a close relationship between the two.) Yet when asked 'Should lesbianism be one of the key issues in the women's movement?' 65 per cent responded affirmatively. (Table 3.6).

Thus, it appears that society is successful in its attempt to separate the personal from the political, sexuality from society and lesbians from women.

None the less, for an individual, the lesbian experience is distinctly related to the experience of women. The individual level is precisely where the awareness of this relationship occurs and from which a feminist framework emerges. With others and in a group context, this type of consciousness has political overtones for lesbians.

They perceive themselves as women and committed to women. But for them to make the necessary link between lesbian politics and women's politics is often a difficult venture. Ironically, in the lesbian group context, their ideas may become blurred. By defining lesbians as primarily 'deviant' and not as 'women', society divorces them not only from itself and mainstream political activity but also from women and feminism (women's politics).

More social lesbians (86 per cent) saw lesbianism as a key 'gay' issue or 'homosexual' issue than as a women's issue (65 per cent) (see Table 3.7). The social process of defining 'gays' or 'homosexuals' as 'deviant' or as an 'out group' has obvious effects upon gays in general and lesbians in particular. Gays' social action area (political context) as well as social label, 'queer', are defined by society. For lesbians as 'gay women', the reactive process and area in which they establish their primary concerns, either with 'gays' or 'women', become socially determined. Society prescribes how and where lesbian activity should emerge and ultimately limits lesbians' political potential and social reaction.

Table 3.7   *Lesbianism and the gay movement – as a key issue?*

QUESTION: 'Should lesbianism be one of the key issues in the gay movement?'

	No.	%
Yes	172	85.6
No	18	9.0
NA	11	5.5
Total	201	100.0

From society's point of view, it is almost as if 'acceptable political activity' (social reaction) for lesbians should develop within and emerge from the general homosexual sub-culture alone. However, for lesbians, involvement in the general homosexual sub-culture (with gay men) renders them inferior. In relationship to gay men, they enact a minimal part within this movement. Roles which they do play tend to further their peculiar oppression as women. Society, therefore, channels lesbians' oppression within this sub-cultural context and tends to dismiss them as not being 'real' women. Thus, we see that the simultaneous rise of homosexual consciousness with feminist consciousness makes conflict inevitable.

In order to collapse the social divisions between homosexual oppression and women's oppression, lesbians struggle to maintain their identity as women. Through this struggle, they expose the way society divides lesbians among themselves and between each other not only in terms of why they are oppressed (as gays or as women) but also why they are lesbian-orientated (born 'sick women' or choosing to be 'social males'). Contradictions run rampant.

Lesbians know that their lives are related to women but as yet many do not know why or in what way. The problem here is that a great majority place themselves, knowingly or unknowingly, within a feminist perspective or take a feminist stance. Yet, while affirming lesbianism as a women's issue, they question its close relationship to feminism. Therefore they deny important structural issues such as patriarchy. These conflicting attitudes may account for lesbian's attributing more priority to their 'issue' as a gay issue than as a women's or feminist issue.

As we shall see with the rise of social lesbianism, their ideas become clearer and possibly develop a more visible and explicit feminist position as well as effective lesbian practice. Nevertheless, all the above findings are of utmost importance and expose a major operating principle for social lesbians. This principle, which I term the 'women before lesbian' factor, points out a crucial element in the contemporary lesbian experience. The experience of lesbianism is definitively related to women. Furthermore, regardless of the social myths which surround them, lesbians view themselves as women first and not as men first. Simply, lesbians are women and are neither 'pseudo-men' nor 'a third sex'. Notwithstanding Freud's theories, social lesbians do not appear as 'penis-envious'. Moreover, as 'structural females' they do not have them. As I pointed out in an earlier discussion, with rare exception, they do not desire them. Ironically stated, lesbians do want to be women. The women before lesbian factor is an abiding reality for the majority of social lesbians.

Lesbianism — viable for women?

Another important finding related to the above also challenges society's views. Social lesbians experience 'meaning', personal validity (i.e. 'I exist') and group viability by living an 'unapproved life'. They demonstrate not only that lesbianism exists but also that women are able effectively to live it out. Its very existence opens up a wide range of possibilities for women. In other words, whether or not social lesbians loudly proclaim their existence, they do demonstrate a possible alternative way of life for women. Viability, even within the confines of the ghetto, maintains a level of social visibility, if only partially or in a marginal way. Through this process, the creation of a social problem is effected. Why is this so? Because possibility becomes a reality and because this reality for women is not recognized as viable *by society*, they create social tensions. As a result, many reject society's label of 'deviant' and carry on with their lives. Society's explicit denial of their viability attempts to impose upon them definitions such as 'queer', 'deviant', 'sick', 'sinful', 'over-sexed', 'pervert' and 'pseudo-man'. These definitions appear to stifle individual viability. However, through human interaction, social lesbians become conscious of the vast implications of these labels. Regardless of the social prejudice against them, they evidence a struggle for social recognition. Also, by creating a viable alternative, they find fulfilment, human comfort and happiness:

> 'It's possible for individual women but not as society sees it. You make it a viable way of life for you and your friends. Those who can do and those who can't. I suppose it may not be viable for all women.'

> 'Of course my life is viable. If I didn't think that I would regard my sexual practices as being perverted. I don't. So I'm open about it.'

> 'It's as viable as any other life. I mean, I sometimes think we ought to re-examine our whole way of looking at society. I mean is marriage viable? Look at it!'

'It's viable for anyone, if they are fulfilled by it, if you really look at yourself and scrutinize yourself and see it's the only way of life for you in which you find happiness.'

Some lesbians feel that lesbianism should be seen as a viable way of life for all women:

'One can only speak from personal experience. Now I've spoken to lots of women about this. They are interested and intrigued. Many women relate to women in a deep way. They are renowned for having women friends, but the patriarchy propaganda is effective. They still think that they need a prick up them.'

'One friend of mine said that she had slept with about 50 or 60 men and never had an orgasm. I pointed out to her, "Can you think of one man who slept with 60 women and who has never had an orgasm?" And she still maintains that she likes men sexually . . . but she is conditioned to believe this. I mean I think lesbianism is a way of life for all women.'

'It's a way of life for all women when they come to realize it and a lot of things. They have to be de-conditioned, I mean. So, it's not a way of life for all women now.'

'Lots of women are really threatened by dykes and no one puts us down like women, like my mother, who is unbelievable and ghastly to me and makes me feel like an animal . . . . Well it reflects so much on their own sexuality. They just can't handle it at all . . . . They live in a straight community and again the whole alienation trip of what men have done to us like, "What have I done wrong?" Well, I think my mother doesn't have a chance.'

These particular attitudes are consistent with an ideology of some lesbians who believe that any women can be a lesbian. In fact, some wear badges which say, 'Any woman can'. The rationale behind this attitude is that all women have the potential to be lesbian but, because of the structure of society, most women are unable to express their lesbianism. However, some expressed doubts about this belief:

'Lesbianism is for all women but it can't be . . . . Straight women are not allowed to be themselves and they realise the wholeness that lesbians have.'

'You know they think it's very intriguing but it's not for them. It makes them think.'

If lesbianism is a viable alternative for all women, this alternative implies a certain degree of choice. However, some express contradictory feelings:

'Women should not be pressurized into thinking that it is not viable and that you have to get a man in the end . . . . But it's not a choice. You can't choose something as basic as lesbianism or heterosexuality.'

'It's the way we are, but here again it's almost like the colour question. All right there's black and white and yellow or red, but we all mix in and I think it should be the same way for lesbians. Why not? Our way is viable.'

Some lesbians justified lesbianism as viable on the sole grounds that one is a woman:

'Well, I'm a woman in society and it's the only way for me. Therefore, it's viable. It has to be. Otherwise I'm not real or not living in a real world.'

'For some women, this all goes back to the question: "Are all women bisexual?" It's definitely very viable for some women, possibly a lot more women than actually believe it. It is an expression of your being and of the person you are. If lesbianism doesn't manifest itself in your behaviour then you're not being that person you are. And if you hide behind heterosexuality or bisexuality then you're not totally expressing yourself.'

In the light of the above comments, it is interesting to see that a large majority of social lesbians felt that lesbianism is a viable way of life for women in society − 17 per cent for all women, 32 per cent for most, 45 per cent for some and 0.5 per cent for few. No one felt that lesbianism was inviable. (See Table 3.8.)

Table 3.8   *Viability of the lesbian experience*

QUESTION: 'Lesbianism is viable for —— in society?'

	No.	%
All women	36	17.9
Most women	65	32.3
Some women	92	45.8
Few women	1	.5
None	—	—
NA	7	3.5
Total	201	100.0

Viability together with the notion of being a women provides lesbians with a firm basis for group identity as well as a sense of strength. As a result, they organize their social lives through a support network which develops on the above basis and which becomes solidified in time.

All these facts — social lesbians' awareness of being women, their commitment to women and the viability of their lives as women — demonstrate that their experiences are definitively related to women and set within a feminist framework.

The non-subservience factor

Another interesting factor which is related to this study is the 'non-subservience factor'. I would contend that it is important not only in terms of this particular study but also for an adequate understanding of lesbianism. Basically, it reveals that despite the various divisions which society creates among social lesbians, there exists one common factor which is observable and which may apply to all social lesbians (and possibly, all lesbians in society). It is that lesbians do not want to be subservient, if only in a sexual context, to a man, some men, most men or all men. Furthermore and related to a previous finding which was highlighted in Chapter 2, lesbians desire to be independent of men in some way: economic, sexual, social, emotional, etc. This finding points out that whether or not social lesbians have been married (23 per cent had), have experienced sexual attractions to a man or men (72 per cent had) or have had a sexual relationship with a man (67 per cent had), they tended to be women who did not desire to be subjected to the sexual – if only in its 'pure', physical form – dominance of a man (see Table 3.9).

Table 3.9   *Lesbians and relationships with men*

QUESTION: 'Have you ever been married?'

	No.	%
Yes	48	23.9
No	149	74.1
NA	4	2.0
Total	201	100.0

QUESTION: 'Have you ever been attracted to a man or men?'

	No.	%
Yes	146	72.6
No	50	24.9
NA	5	2.5
Total	201	100.0

QUESTION: 'Have you ever had sex with a man?'

	No.	%
Yes	135	67.2
No	61	30.3
NA	5	2.5
Total	201	100.0

These findings may be surprising to some readers. However, they do call into question social images of lesbians as being repulsed by men. If such a large majority (73 per cent) of social lesbians have had hetero-sexual feelings and more than half (67 per cent) have actually experi-enced 'heterosexual sex', what then accounts for their lesbianism? Are lesbians really perverts? If so, why haven't they been consistently so? Do they really hate men? If so, why are they attracted to men or furthermore, why did they have sex with their supposed 'hated enemies' at some times? Obviously these issues raise many questions.

Let us not forget that lesbianism, contrary to society's view, does not necessitate general hostility towards men. In fact, only 27 per cent of the social lesbians in the sample felt that they had hostile feelings or hostile attitudes towards men; 38 per cent felt accepting, while 29 per cent felt indifferent to men (see Table 3.10).

Table 3.10 *Social lesbians' feelings towards men*

QUESTION: 'What are your attitudes or feelings towards men?'

	No.	%
Hostile	54	26.9
Indifferent	59	29.4
Accepting	77	38.3
NA	11	5.5
Total	201	100.0

It appears that lesbians are not generally hostile to men and are either indifferent or accepting towards them (68 per cent). However, regardless of these attitudes, lesbianism objectively challenges a male-orientated society in which men are dominant and primary and where women remain subservient and secondary. Lesbianism is a reaction against society and women's position within it:

'Lesbianism is an empathy with women but mainly because it's a reaction against men and society or a male-defined society.'

'Looking back on it . . . . In the beginning when I became a lesbian I wouldn't be able to tell you why. I mean I wouldn't have realized it at the time. But I would say I didn't want to be subservient. I wanted to be my own self, my own independent self and I always got on better with women. And I should think what probably helped me along was not having any brothers. So I wasn't used to men. I know women better.'

'I think that basically if society weren't structured the way it is, that if the advantages weren't given to men and if women weren't brainwashed, I suppose the role of childbearing and feeding would give women a primary social role and maybe even an economic one too. I think of my husband. When I left him, poor ——. At the point in which I buggered off, which I did very gently, he said, "I really have no role without providing for you. But, you don't need me to

provide for you . . . I've done everything society said I should do
but you've shown me by up and going that in fact, I'm not as
primary as I'm supposed to be – just sitting here beating
my chest." '

'A lesbian is not dependent upon men for sex or money. She's
already not necessarily competing with men but she has to be self-
sufficient in those two very central areas.'

The non-subservience factor illustrates the varying degrees of independence that social lesbians experience in relationship to men. I would
contend that this factor emerges from the process in which sexuality is
structured by society and how it organizes power on both the individual and social levels. If a woman is confronted with a subservient
social position and secondary function and if she is aware of their
implications, she may reject being an 'acceptable' women in society's
eyes. This finding points out the crucial structural problems and objective social issues which confront all women – lesbians and straight
women alike – and which determine the existence of a patriarchal
capitalist social order. This order imposes upon women 'acceptable'
social definitions which are explicitly bound up with a 'subservient-
orientation', a secondary social function (reproduction) and a lower
social position, economically, politically, socially and sexually.

For a lesbian, the desire not to be subservient exposes a variety of
contradictions. As a 'structural female', able to reproduce, she ultimately rejects the social implication of this role – economic and sexual
dependence upon a man within the structure of marriage and the
family context. For society, her rejection reveals a gross inconsistency
between her physical ability or 'structural femaleness' and her, albeit
non-existence in society's eyes, 'social femaleness' – society's exhorta-
tion to be feminine, passive, dependent upon men. Society says, 'You
are a woman and therefore you *must* be female!' The lesbian responds
by saying, 'Yes, I am a woman, but I will not be "female" (dependent)
and obviously, I'm not a man. I may appear as "male" (independent)
but I am aware of myself as a woman.' Because it is difficult for society
to place the lesbian into a neat box and because of lesbians' resistence
to a rigid framework, confusion arises. Society becomes perplexed.

Lesbians and change: a potential social force?

Initially in this chapter, we examined how lesbianism as a social phenomenon is changing in light of three 'lesbian' views. At this time, I would
contend that, as operating principles, the women before lesbian factor
and the non-subservience factor do accelerate this development of
lesbianism as a social phenomenon and are primarily located within the
second stage, social lesbianism. These factors create a potential social
force and provide the basis for an ideological view of lesbianism. Con-
current with the creation of a social force, social lesbians experience a
specific lesbian awareness, as socially-orientated, and a particular group
consciousness — pre-political. These two elements, individual awareness
and group consciousness, provide the basis for lesbian politics. But, how
does this basis become established? How does it manifest itself and,
furthermore, maintain itself?

In order to answer thoroughly the above questions, we should
examine the chronological development of social lesbians' awareness in
terms of the initial points of entry into experience which society types
as 'lesbian'; lesbians' subsequent perception of those experiences, and
society's 'soft-negative' ascription of the deviant label, lesbian.

Table 3.11   *Social lesbians and the age factor* (N = 201)

	Age	First attraction	First 'lesbian sex'	Definition age
Mean	30.3	13.1	21.8	22.6
Median	28.3	12.8	20.4	21.5
SD	10.1	6.7	7.0	7.6

Mean =   the average of set of values (in this case, age values).
Median =   the age above which half the values lie and below which the
remaining half lie.
SD =   Standard Deviation. This has nothing to do with the process
of becoming 'deviant'. It is a statistical calculation which is a
measure of dispersion. It represents the square root of the
variance which is the average of the squares of all the
deviations about the mean. Basically, it tells us how
numbers of sets of values 'deviate' from the mean.

For the purpose of developing a sense of chronology, it is useful to
examine three moments in time. They are: the age of attraction, when
a lesbian was first attracted to women; the age when a lesbian first

experienced sex with a woman, and the age of self-definition, when a lesbian actually accepted the social label 'lesbian' for herself. These ages prove to be interesting because they reveal that lesbian awareness does not appear as an 'essence', a 'static thing', 'something' one is or 'a fixed entity' one is 'born with'. Lesbian awareness and resultant lesbian consciousness seem to grow and develop along with the awareness of being a woman (see Table 3.11).

The mean age of the social lesbians was 30 years of age. On average, they were initially attracted to women when they were around 13 years of age; had their first sexual experiences with a woman ('lesbian sex') at around 21 years of age and defined themselves as 'lesbian' at around 22 years of age. Therefore, it appears that the majority of social lesbians have been attracted to other women for 17 years. Yet, in the majority of cases, they did not actively live out this attraction until they were 21 years old. These findings point out that while being attracted to women for more than half of their present life-time (57 per cent of their 30-year span), most have been 'active lesbians' sexually for only one-third of their present life-time, since they were 21 years old (30 per cent of their 30-year span). Furthermore, the majority took upon themselves the label 'lesbian' only after their initial sexual experience.

What could account for this 'dormant period' when they were attracted to other women and did not live it out? If lesbianism is supposed to be an innate characteristic, why do lesbians take not only two-thirds of their present life-time to find it out but also the same amount of time actually to accept this label for themselves?

This dormant period between the ages of 13 and 21 is the adolescent stage of development for a woman. I would contend that it is a time characterized by heightened social pressure to conform to 'the acceptable female role', which, as we have seen, many had done. Going out with boys and men as well as establishing sexual relationships with them become the 'order of the day'. To reiterate a point, many lesbians have experienced not only women but also men (73 per cent) as sexually attractive; 67 per cent have actually had 'heterosexual sex'. Possibly it is during this dormant period that they become 'heterosexually active'. After all, through their awareness of society's expectations for them as young women, they may find it easier to be heterosexual-orientated than lesbian-orientated. Lesbian fantasies along with lesbian practice tend to remain in abeyance. As lesbians reject being moulded by society and develop beyond adolescence, they find it easier to choose for themselves their sexual orientation and their 'acceptable' social label, acceptable for themselves, that is.

From the above, we should assume that her first experience of lesbian sex is very important for a young woman. It may propel her into a life-long commitment to women. One lesbian who had been married described how she had developed a sense of awareness about herself. She did not have any sexual experiences with a woman until her twelfth year of marriage. Yet this initial experience brought with it a series of responses which culminated in a lesbian label:

'In order to express some sort of sexual preference for women I had to develop a tremendous sense of self-awareness that I, in fact, existed in my own right, that I had integrity, that I had a right to exist in an affirmative way and that the things society told me were completely erroneous. So I had a tremendous sense of self-awareness to do what I've done . . . to break up a really good marriage with a nice man who I had much in common with . . . . The sense of self-awareness came first. Then out of that came lesbianism in an individual sense then a group one.'

It is illuminating to see how some lesbians recall their initial experience. One older lesbian recounted that it seemed quite humorous to her now. Having emerged from the traditional view of lesbianism, her example appears to maintain society's stereotype of lesbian sexual initiation, that of seduction by an older woman:

'It was a very funny one. I was about 14 and I was seduced by my governess. She was beautiful. She was married to a French doctor. It happened after she left me. Of course, I was at school at the time. She went over to Paris to live but she came over here to see her folks and it was suggested that it might be a good idea if she and I had a couple of weeks holiday together for old time's sake and we did. As I said she seduced me and of course, she got very frightened and said she'd never do it again. She sort of begged me and pleaded with me and cried, you know, not to tell my mother. Well, I would never tell my mother. But, anyways, that's how it was.'

Rejecting society's view that 'lesbianism is unnatural behaviour', one lesbian describes the opposite — her experience was 'very natural':

'The person I started having an affair with was someone that seemed

to be a perfectly average sort of person. Not the sort of person
that there was anything sordid about. Previously, I thought these
things were sordid and maybe nasty. But this woman was
particularly the opposite – just a normal person. She didn't look
particularly butch or anything like that . . . . It all seemed very
nice. It was nice and all very natural.'

An older lesbian in her late 50s spoke about the ambivalence which
characterized her first experience: 'I thought, "I am twisted, dirty,
disgusting, perverted . . . ." But I knew that the experience was wonderful for me.'

On the personal or individual level, the transformation from an
'acceptable woman' (in society's eyes) to an unacceptable woman is
produced. Usually at this point in time, one also becomes aware of an
'outside-group': lesbian sub-culture. This awareness creates the potential for lesbian group consciousness. In effect, groups of women aware
of being lesbian-orientated organize together socially on the basis of
their respective awareness. Through social lesbianism, changes in oneself
occur simultaneously with changes in others. Thus a group perspective
develops. Organization with others makes 'formal' potential social
challenge. Through this process, social change on the structural level of
society is possible. Here, the implication is that the development of
lesbian consciousness not only effects change for an individual and on
the group level but is also affected by any altering of the position of
women in society. This becomes clearer by analysing lesbians' ideas
about change. In other words, do lesbians' ideas about themselves
change over time (Table 3.12)?

Table 3.12   *Social lesbians and change*

QUESTION: 'Have your ideas about lesbianism and your definition of
lesbianism changed over time?'

	No.	%
Yes	165	82.1
No	36	17.9
Total	201	100.0

A large majority (82 per cent) expressed the belief that their ideas
had changed. Why is this so? I would propose that lesbians meet with

change because of their intense involvement with the lesbian experience, as primarily women-committed, and within the social lesbian frame- work, as primarily group-orientated. In other words, their ideas change over time more through their particular lesbian viewpoint (as feminist- based) and their relationship to a group identity (social lesbianism) than through any other relevant social or psychological factors. Sixty-seven per cent felt that they had experienced change in this way (Table 3.13).

Table 3.13 *Why social lesbians change*

QUESTION: 'Why do you think you have changed?'

	No.	% of 201
The lesbian experience	135	67.2
Women's movement	70	34.8
Gay movement	77	38.3
Group therapy	7	3.4
Individual therapy	13	6.46

Obviously, the social label 'lesbian' does affect one's self-image as well as creates change. If a lesbian comes out, she is up against a whole range of social myths, biases and expectations which define this nega- tive label. In an immediate group sense a group framework justifies the label, cushions the struggle and facilitates the coming-out process. Perhaps this framework makes it easier for society to 'come clean' or to reveal its biases. However, it may also escalate the conflict by creating more social tensions.

Earlier we saw that in comparison with homosexuality for men, lesbianism is viewed as secondary, non-threatening and not important, such as the category 'women' in a male-orientated society. Ultimately, it is seen as non-existent. Therefore, society's reaction to lesbianism is consistent with these views. Seemingly it takes a 'softer' negative approach to lesbians than to gay men. In terms of this particular study, the findings correspond to society's approach — 56 per cent of the social lesbians were made to feel 'bad', 'deviant', perverse, evil or sinful by those who knew them to be lesbian (Table 3.14).

Presumably, if society's approach and reaction to lesbianism was more harsh, more lesbians, possibly all of the 86 per cent who have a tendency to be 'out', would have responded 'yes' rather than 'no' to the question in Table 3.14. Also, these findings point out that being out, which the majority in varying degrees are, may not be as 'bad', 'unrewarding', 'stigmatizing' or 'negative', as society tells the lesbian. Perhaps society and not the lesbian is caught unawares. Maybe, sexuality is no longer a private issue.

Table 3.14   *Social lesbians and the 'softer' negative approach*

QUESTION: 'Were you ever made to feel bad, deviant, etc. . . . by those who know you to be a lesbian?'

	No.	%
Yes	114	56.7
No	81	40.3
NA	6	3.0
Total	201	100.0

In fact, many lesbians (65 per cent) responded that people to whom they are 'out' accept them or have positive feelings towards them (Table 3.15);19 per cent responded that people were indifferent, while only 8 per cent responded that people were hostile. These findings expose unfounded social beliefs and create a lesson, still to be learned, for both the lesbian and society. For the lesbian, unlike she imagines, may 'come out' without necessarily producing the negative or hostile responses she imagines in others. Coming out usually involves struggling with feelings which are projected from society such as 'You are a bad person', 'You are a pervert'. However, being out or open about one's lesbianism does not tend to create hostility or negativity from others. For society, to make one's private life a public issue or one's sexual orientation social knowledge is a matter for scorn. Yet, this is possible

Table 3.15   *Social lesbians and people's reaction*

QUESTION: 'How do people react to you when they know you to be a lesbian?'

	No.	%
Accepting	131	65.2
Indifferent	39	19.4
Hostile	17	8.5
NA	14	7.0
Total	201	100.0

without social opprobrium or getting people's backs up. It appears that the only thing that lesbians and society have to fear is fear itself!

From the above discussion in this chapter, we see that social lesbianism effects development on the personal, group and societal levels. As a relatively new phenomenon, it seems to be developing at a rapid rate. In effect, it may become a social force for lesbians. However, when society's dominant ideas separate social lesbians from each other, this stifles an ideological view as well as the potential for social change. As a result, the growth of 'lesbian politics' becomes stunted in a divisive process. Arbitrary divisions set off reactions and social organization which subsequently have effects upon lesbian consciousness. The following chapters will describe in detail this process and its results. We will discuss the two groups of social lesbians along with their respective elements.

4 'Sick, but not sorry' *vs* 'sorry, but not sick': the born lesbian and the self-chosen lesbian

As with all social phenomena, lesbianism is changing. In the midst of this transition, traditional ideas from the past linger on, while new ideas are created. Old aspects of lesbianism merge with newer forms of ideas, expanding attitudes as well as changing values. Inroads for the future are continually being made. Within this complex process, threads of historical consistency become barely visible. Yet as the fabric of lesbianism unfolds before us, we are able to trace a single strand which runs through the lesbian experience and which ultimately connects the total struggle both within itself and to society. This strand, a crucial historical link, is the awareness and development of a lesbian group identity.

The emergence of social lesbianism: tradition vs ideology

The data presented in this book is based on the four-year study of lesbians in London I describe in the Introduction. Initially, a sample was taken from two distinct yet similar groups within the lesbian population. The existence of both groups illustrates quite clearly the emergence of social lesbianism. One group, Sappho, indicates vestiges of the past, having a somewhat traditional view of lesbianism, while the other group, the Conference lesbians, present newer ideas with hints of ideology.[1] Each respective group is neither totally bound by tradition nor totally directed towards ideology. Rather, as we shall see, a spectrum of views is represented within each group as well as within the total group of social lesbians. As predominantly social-orientated, these lesbians appear to have a pre-political consciousness. In other words, they are not yet totally aware of their social position as lesbians. However, social lesbianism does not preclude stages of awareness which are either apolitical or political. In effect, the Sappho group appears to develop from an apolitical to a pre-political consciousness, while Conference lesbians seem to shift from a pre-political consciousness to a political one.

Emerging from tradition, Sappho has encountered many changes within the lesbian struggle. It was originally formed about seven years ago by a group of lesbians who became disenchanted with society's view of lesbianism as well as its treatment of them as psychiatric scapegoats.[2] This small group which formed Sappho began to organize regular meetings for themselves and for other lesbians. Gradually, a larger group was formed and it included more lesbians. Weekly meetings were set up within a bar atmosphere. This appeared to provide lesbians with an environment in which they were able not only to relax but also to 'be themselves'. Eventually, the publication of *Sappho*, a lesbian magazine, was effected. It became obvious that group awareness was growing. This group awareness, in turn, helped to establish Sappho's identity as a particular lesbian organization. Today the magazine prides itself on being the most widely-read lesbian magazine in Europe. As well as promoting the group's work, which is primarily directed towards establishing a sense of lesbian awareness, the journal helped to expand communication networks between lesbians. The aims were and still are to reach those who are fearful of coming out, even within an 'all-lesbian' context (in Sappho meetings for example). Sappho therefore appeals to both the out and the closet lesbians. But, on the whole, it still maintains an air of secrecy.

The Conference lesbians represent some of the lesbians who attended a Lesbian National Conference in Bristol during 1976. The Conference was formed by lesbians who perhaps felt that to organize in a manner similar to Sappho was not sufficient if a group desired to challenge society. Thus, they attempted to publicize the lesbian issue by getting lesbians together in a social context which was predisposed to political action. In this way, a more explicit reaction against society takes place. Simply, group awareness develops in contrast to society rather than as an appendage to it. In the end, the Conference which was attended by various groups from all over the country raised important issues related to lesbianism, for example, feminism, gay politics, bisexuality, lesbian mothers, wages for lesbians, abortion, coming out, and so on. Although limited by a three-day existence, the Conference effected long-range goals and the Conference ideas branched out over time. Other groups which were smaller in size emerged from it, built up networks of communication and re-worked similar 'seed' ideas.

Both the Sappho lesbians and the Conference lesbians have certain recognizable elements which create social lesbianism. Yet, the existence of both groups exposes tensions among social lesbians. An awareness of these tensions is important for our understanding of social lesbianism. Each group within the lesbian ghetto reflects roughly particular differences in terms of their emergence from traditional lesbianism: the reason why they are lesbians; their notion of the 'sexual' as being either a private matter or a public issue, and their stakes within the system.

Why am I a lesbian?

Society's traditional view of lesbianism causes a split between both groups of social lesbians. This view and all that it entails affects their subsequent self-perception of the reasons why they are lesbian-orientated.

Ideas about lesbianism filter through the dominant sexual ideology. Therefore, they are consistent with the creation of the category 'sexual' in society. Lesbians along with heterosexuals suffer from the oppressive features of essentialism.

As a result, some social lesbians view their lesbianism as an 'entity' or an 'object of human nature'. Believing that 'it' is a purely sexual 'thing', these lesbians manifest the 'sick, but not sorry' syndrome. Having emerged from the isolation of the past, they, in varying degrees, placidly accept traditional images of lesbians as sick, genetically inferior, hormonally imbalanced, and so on. As a result, sick but not sorry types have a tendency to feel that they are 'born lesbians'. The option for a relative degree of choice of lesbianism in a highly complex social order becomes clouded over. Viewing themselves as a 'third sex', they accept orthodox definitions and thus create around themselves an aura of a fixed state or a static, personal condition. Although these ideas and definitions are changing, they help to form the initial impression that lesbianism is a sexual preference. Yet, as we have seen, this 'preference' implies a primary commitment to and empathy with all women. Because they are 'socially deformed', the born lesbians usually attempt to hide their 'deformity' — 'After all, the sexual is private.' Or born lesbians accept 'it' as another part of themselves, like an appendage:

'After all, yes, the sexual is private, but I can't help the way I am. I don't want to hide it. So, society better accept me as one of its unfortunates. I had no choice in the matter. Why should I be punished?'

Some born lesbians explained it in this way:

'Well, there is such a thing as a born lesbian. I am a born lesbian. I am born a lesbian because since the day I was born I sort of knew that I was different. Obviously, I didn't even know what the word was, but I knew that I was different. And so far as I'm concerned this happened either at conception or in the womb or something. But there are a lot of people who think that they are lesbians. Of course, there's a big, big difference from being a man-hater, which I think or I hate to say a lot of the young ones are, and being a lesbian, a true lesbian . . . . A true lesbian is a born lesbian. There is just no other answer or way out and that's it. You just have to learn to live with it. I'm very lucky. I've never had problems because I've always known. I think I've been very lucky.'

'People are getting more enlightened now that they are getting prepared to accept us as a third sex . . . . I'm sure they do.'

'I am as I am because I am. I was born this way. I can't help it. Because if I think even now only a few of us would say quite literally, "I am glad to be gay". I am because I'm nice and old. I've enjoyed my life and I'm quite sure that there are other women who still prefer to be heterosexuals because it's an easier way of life. But here again, this is improving you know.'

'I had very much known what I was but didn't know a word for it. When someone told me the word, lesbian, then I saw myself as a lesbian ever since.'

Although the sorry but not sick types also emerge from tradition, they challenge these views. Their self-perception differs markedly from the sick but not sorry lesbians. The 'Sorry' reject not only society's stereotypes of lesbianism but also the 'illness, perversion or disease' syndrome of the 'Sick'. For the former group, lesbianism is a choice which is grounded in a variety of factors, social, psychological, emotional and political. As a result, they are 'self-chosen' lesbians and tend to see lesbianism as a total commitment to women or as a way of life rather than as a sexual preference. Some seek social acceptance and/or recognition by actively challenging society's previous explanations. The proposed element of choice confuses the lesbian issue:

'Whether society views it as a way of life, we have chosen it. Society thinks we are missing out on an awful lot. Society at the moment can only accept it as something which is a substitute for something else. Almost always it has to be related to some traumatic experience in one's past life. There has to be some terrible occurrence in one's childhood, something lacking in one's upbringing or something bad which happened to them and is accountable for the fact that one is now a lesbian.'

'If a girl gets raped when she is 3 years old that would explain to society her reason for being a lesbian. Society is always looking for that "get out", that explanation for why lesbians as women can't even have any sexual connection with men. There must be some area in her life which will explain it to society. It just can't be that a person has grown up to prefer women to men. There has to be some explanation. For me, that's wrong. I look at myself. I've chosen it so somebody is wrong. I think it's society.'

'You must choose this way of life. It's different because you're gearing yourself against what society expects of you or the constraints society has put upon you. The fact that a heterosexual relationship is normal and anything else is abnormal and tolerated to one degree or another. If it's not a heterosexual relationship there, it's not right. Something must explain it – some hangup. A lesbian's life is a different way of life because you're only prepared to commit yourself to another woman, if you have to commit yourself at all. Hence, you're going against the constraints put upon you by society. It's a different way of life.'

For all social lesbians, the element of change plays a large part in establishing a group awareness. Yet often this element, although present in the group context, does not filter through to one's personal experience. As a result, some social lesbians express contradictory feelings about changes in their lesbian definition.

Born lesbians, while upholding a 'static view' of lesbianism, accept their lives as changing and/or related to new ideas:

'Yes my ideas have changed because I used to think of it, as most
women did, as a purely sexual thing. I think of it more as a complete
way of life. It's not that I have thought this out but it's so obvious.
I mean my whole way of life has changed. I want it to change. It
makes me much happier. All right, I've accepted the fact I can live
this way.'

'My ideas haven't changed but my approach to relationships has
changed a tremendous amount.'

'Lesbianism affects attitudes to everyone in society. If you know
what society has told you is lies then it affects your whole way of
looking at politics, economics . . . . We have a lesbian perspective
on things like the way society governs.'

Similarly, self-chosen lesbians tend implicitly to uphold change. Yet,
some contradict this implicit belief and appear to negate views which
are related to change, growth or development. Some confuse these
notions:

'The idea hasn't changed. It's grown.'

'As I said from the very start, I saw it as women-directed but I
define it in terms of the sex aspect. I guess I see it very much as I'm
really primarily a woman and secondarily a lesbian.'

Still, other self-chosen lesbians spoke of their struggle to change. It
appears that overwhelming changes sometimes occur through set-backs,
lapses into traditional ways or in a regressive manner:

'The whole thing snowballs. Definitely, when I was younger I used
to feel confident or sure of myself. At 20 or 21, everything had
gone again. I had a lapse back into my old ways. It was a while
back. This was only because I wasn't being honest with myself
which meant being honest with everyone else. There were certain
things I was holding back but my awareness is up there now. It's
just amazing so that in 6 months' time in a year's time there will
be many more dykes who think the same way.'

'I ask questions about roles as a type of awareness. I don't have to push them off because I have been conditioned into them. I've got to unlearn all of these processes that I've learned through the gay ghetto and things.'

'The first time I heard of gay anything I had been living in — with a woman. I travelled around England for a bit, then I came to —. I got a job as a singer in a bar. My head barmaid was bisexual. She rang a lot of her lesbian friends – 'Come and see what I've got behind the bar.' I thought it was marvellous all those gay people standing around in bars arms around each other – dancing, feelings getting high . . . . Gay boys were so funny. I picked up all of their habits and ugh, ghastly traits and camp voices . . . . I picked up the whole lot. I couldn't see through it. It was a sort of kaleidoscope. I was overawed . . . went to every party. It took me a long time to see the falseness of it all and how much of a ghetto it was. I go back occasionally to sell tickets for discos, but I don't really go near too much.'

Regardless of any resistence to change or lack of change on a personal level, a large majority in both groups and among corresponding types of lesbians manifest a transition in the lesbian experience. Objectively, this change establishes them within a social lesbian framework as well as at a pre-political stage of awareness. Although the total sample of social lesbians appeared to be generally receptive to change, some resistance was evident. The Sappho lesbians tended to be of the sick but not sorry syndrome as well as to include a majority of born lesbians. In effect, this group indicated more resistance to change than the Conference lesbians. The latter group represented the sorry but not sick syndrome and was composed primarily of self-chosen lesbians (see Table 4.1).

Table 4.1   *Lesbians and change*

QUESTION: 'Have your views of lesbianism developed over time?'

	Sick No.	%		Sorry No.	%
Yes	74	74	Yes	91	90.1
No.	26	26	No	10	9.9
Total	100	100	Total	101	100.0

It was interesting that for the majority of lesbians in both groups a transformation from traditional views was apparent. This indicates that the development of a group awareness does effect change whether or not the notion of change is perceived on the personal level.

Private or public notion of sexuality?

For a lesbian, either her private or public notion of sexuality is affected by how she views lesbianism, as being more of a sexual preference than as an identity related to women or vice versa; how she copes with her views – in a predominantly social or political way; how she interacts as a social lesbian, either sheltering her secret or proclaiming it publicly, and ultimately, how open she is in society about her lesbianism, for example, is she closeted or out?

These clear-cut divisions are made in order to illustrate how social lesbians cope with the dominant sexual ideology. In reality, however, these divisions are not usually as clear-cut as I have indicated. The lesbian struggle, and the spectrum of social activity, are built up not only within the context of society but also within the field of group practice *vis à vis* the experiences of individual lesbians. As a result, lesbians establish a variety of fronts throughout society. Primarily, these fronts represent some form of social reaction, regardless of the specific level or stage of awareness. Yet, the tension between a privatized life and a public one appears as the phenomenon unfolds before us:

'I am not sure that I have really opened up my secret and private life to anybody else. I am still afraid of this "not nice area". Whatever it is, causing someone I am very fond of or close to to not like me, I don't know.'

'Lesbianism impinges upon areas in your life in which it's not relevant. Like if I'm teaching certain subjects I don't think I could bring it up unless it's during break time. If someone asked me, "Are you married?", I'd say, "Well, actually, I'm gay." I would bring it up then.'

'They find it threatening when we're public. I mean we have to define society and the western world as a male-dominated society. They are definitely threatened by us. What I find a joke about our

society is it's all very artsy fartsy specialized highly technical people
– all educated in lots of ways . . . but the most basic taboos and
feelings still act out in society which is meant to be sophisticated.
It's a joke. This proves to me what a sick society we live in because
they're all writing about this and that in papers, about literature,
poems, symbolism, talking about sexual responses of dogs. All of
them, as if they're really superior but still their reaction to lesbians
just shows what a gut reaction they still have. They are meant to be
so superior.'

'Society's reaction to lesbians is one of complete fear that manifests
itself in trying to heap degradation on lesbians. The saddest thing is
that women, straight women, hate dykes because it threatens them
and their role as a result of these men. I've had a feeling recently
(another thing about being a lesbian is that I trust my feelings more
than I did before when I was straight) as if we are now the germ
of what's going to happen. If the world is not destroyed before we
can get it going there is a possibility that it may be a matriarchal
culture. It's almost as if we are the beginnings of it – there are these
pockets of resistance to this fucking male society.'

'At quite an early age, I had what would then be called homosexual
feelings. I couldn't be out in the open with them, at the same time
in my mind I definitely was.'

'When I was about 14, I supported homosexual rights. I read
anything about homosexuality. Of course, I was very secretive. One
of the first things that ever came out was a little book written by a
Quaker about sex. It was controversial because it said homosexuality
was quite a natural thing. It affected me a lot at the time. When I
went to university, I was still conscious of gay society. It was hard.
In my mind, I couldn't do it myself. I felt emotionally inadequate.
I needed to prove I was heterosexual. It was a split between an
intellectual thing and a personal thing. I approved of it but
emotionally for the people around me it just wasn't on for me to
invite some woman to bed. Therefore, I related to men then I
gradually changed.'

'Well, when I first thought, "Oh, I must be a lesbian", I was scared.
I didn't tell anybody. I mean it was strange.'

'When I was in my first year at university, there were a few women
who were dykes. People kind of threw rocks at them. I mean it
wasn't proper to come out even then. Everybody used to throw
rocks at them, boys and girls. They were obviously typed as weird,
bad, creepy.'

Regardless of whether or not society appears to be taking more
'liberal' views on sexuality in general and lesbianism in particular,
society does oppress lesbians. The existence of social lesbianism, the
development of increased group activity and of a growing group identity, helps to illustrate a potentially threatening posture. If the gaps in
understanding are filled between society and sexuality, the realization
of impending doom materializes. Society knows this to be inevitable.
Therefore, privacy must be upheld at the expense of those who may or
may not comprehend the vast implications of 'sexual secrecy'. Scores of
women are told not to 'get their skirts ruffled' or not to be disturbed
by those who are not 'real women' like themselves. A rejected male-
orientated society fights back against lesbianism. The dominant ideology filters through to men who have the power to experience this
refusal of their potency — whether sexual, economic, political or social.
'Liberal' society's acceptance of lesbianism runs amiss. In the face of a
threat to its established order and structure, society's peace treaty,
'Lesbianism is acceptable, if it is private', however alluring or inviting
it may appear to be, is ultimately broken: 'But you are still "deviant" '.
  Society snaps back into consciousness and hangs on to tradition. In a
diatribe against lesbians, ideology-makers glibly spin out ideas which
justify the broken truce:

'We all know that women are made for the home. As ideal mothers,
they are rooted in their relationships with men and in the family.
Women should continue to be our cheap source of labour. Sexuality,
sex, sexual issues relate more to women than to men. After all,
women are the ones who have to be sexy if they want men and more
importantly, if they want men's babies. Lesbians are different. They
aren't women and they must be hidden from view. Sexual problems
are personal ones. They are deviations from our norms and values.
They are sins. Lesbians, puffs, queers, etc. don't fit in. So they'd
better hide themselves away from us. Political? Sex can never be
political. It's outrageous for anyone to think that. The personal, sex,
can never be a political issue. Politics means how we govern. We

must keep up these distinctions or we'll fall apart and anarchy will reign.'

Social lesbians, as well as many heterosexuals and gay men, may fall for these ideas in varying degrees. Although objectively challenging society, the practice of social lesbianism may collude with society. While making their lives more open, some social lesbians do not view themselves as being political. Yet, for some who are moving towards politics, remaining secretive in certain areas of their lives is not a contradiction.

In the total sample, the majority are politically orientated (63.7 per cent). However, politically-minded lesbians may or may not make important links between their personal or private lives and their lesbian politics or social lives.

The majority in each group of social lesbians expose a particular tendency in relationship to lesbian politics. The sick but not sorry type tend not to view themselves as political (only 39 per cent felt they were political). The majority of the sorry but not sick type (88 per cent) assume a political stance. (See Table 4.2.)

Table 4.2   *Social lesbians and lesbian politics*

QUESTION: Are you political or not?

	Total No.	%	Sick No.	%	Sorry No.	%
Yes	128	63.7	39	39	89	88.9
No	73	36.3	61	61	12	11.9
Total	201	100.0	100	100.0	101	100.0

In this particular sample, the level of resistance to society's view that 'lesbianism should not be political' is 63 per cent. In coping with their resistance, social lesbians express a variety of views. Nevertheless, they expose a group identity with many conflicts and at a pre-political stage of awareness:

'I'm sure you know I was a first founding member of ——. I don't go to political meetings because I'm not a political animal. Quite honestly, it's not my scene. This is where a lot of aggression comes in where it spoils our movement. It's just my view. I go to the discos.

I have my personal friends. Well, they do belong to ——. Most of them I have known and met because of this organization. What really worries me is that aggression only breeds aggression. This is one thing we do not want. It never used to be like that.'

'Some disagreements we've had here [in her specific group context] mean that we don't see some women again. That is really sad. Because I feel strongly that one has to hold one's feelings about being a political lesbian. If other women don't accept it, they'll have to get out and do their own thing. The thing about being a lesbian is that it is political. If you see yourself as a non-political lesbian, you're falling into a trap of a male-dominated society that's put you down ever since you've had the first inkling that you were a lesbian. Because you can't tell me there isn't any woman who hasn't been freaked out by the fears that she was a lesbian.'

'There's a big difference from being a man-hater, which a lot of these young women's libbers are, and a lesbian. The women's movement is a wonderful thing but I'm a little bit afraid of the hostility that comes from within it and from it. It won't help us. In fact, it's going to put people's backs up against us. But, I don't think as far as the women's movement is concerned that it matters whether we're lesbians or not.'

'You don't have to be self-righteous but you can keep to your own political line. You have to realize: everyone is on a different level if you like. There are probably lots of women who you talk with who will never be political, they can't be bothered.'

For social lesbians, the potential for lesbian politics runs high as they begin to integrate their ideas, life-styles and self-definitions within the field of social reaction. In other words, lesbians not only react against society but against each other. In a state of constant flux, the move towards lesbian consciousness and political practice becomes a reality. Although lesbians struggle with 'tradition', they move forward if only to regress yet again. Thwarted by society and their personal confrontations within it, they fearlessly or fearfully may attempt the leap from the personal to the political. Along with the privatized, individualized view of lesbianism, their degradation ceases to be permanent. As women, they establish their priorities and make them visible. The overwhelming presence of the 'woman before lesbian' factor crystallizes this process.

Within this context, it is interesting to note that social lesbians tend to de-personalize the lesbian definition for lesbians as a group. Consistent with this group orientation, they break down barriers among themselves as well as between themselves and other women. Although, at first glance, the findings in Table 4.3 may seem contradictory, they are compatible with not only where social lesbians' priorities lie, more as women than as lesbians, but also with how they eventually sense these priorities, within a group or as individuals.

Table 4.3   *Definition of lesbianism*

QUESTION: How do you define lesbianism?

	Total No.	%	Sick No.	%		Sorry No.	%	
As a sexual preference	60	29.9	35	35		25	24.8	
A counter-identity for women	6	3.0	3	3	64% shift from tradition	3	3.0	69% shift from tradition
A total way of life for women	90	44.8	37	37		53	52.5	
An alternative way of life for women	38	18.9	24	24		14	13.9	
NA	7	3.5	1	1		6	5.9	
Total	201	100.0	100	100		101	100.0	

On the one hand, if lesbianism is defined as a 'total way of life for women', 'a counter-identity for women' or 'an alternative way of life for women', a lesbian appears to strengthen her feminist roots, to de-personalize the lesbian label and to opt for a type of group awareness. On the other hand, if the traditional notion of 'sexual preference' is chosen, the effect of one's origins, from traditional views of the past become evident. This latter choice further isolates the lesbian phenomenon from the group experience.

Surprisingly or not, both types of lesbian shift away from tradition (64 per cent of the 'Sick' and 69 per cent of the 'Sorry'). Although the former group may appear as more bound to tradition than the latter, both swing towards collective awareness – the crux of social lesbianism. The following example illustrates the effects of this transition upon a

particular lesbian. Ambiguity and uncertainty emerge, as the definition
of lesbianism changes:

> 'Lesbians are women who have a sexual preference for women. I'm
> not sure whether it's exclusive or whether it's just a matter of
> sexual preference. In other words, I'm not sure if one talks in terms
> of putting exclusive preference on women in every way.'

In different ways, other social lesbians express similar priorities:

> 'To me, a lesbian is now a woman who loves other women — purely
> and simply that.'

> 'I once defined a lesbian as a women whose meaningful relationships
> are with other women, which means women are going to be more
> important. A woman is going to occupy the same place in one's life
> as a man would occupy in the life of a straight woman.'

Once a lesbian achieves the 'status' of social lesbian, how then does
she interact with others? Does she perpetuate an air of secrecy or does
she cast all cares to the wind? As social-orientated, is she fearful of
frequent interaction with other lesbians or does she immerse herself
within the shifting waters of the ghetto? Having developed a pre-
political disposition, does she regress to old ways or former consciousness or does she push on to develop new forms of consciousness and
lesbian social reaction? The answer to these questions will not be
simple 'yes' or 'no'. In whatever ways they are raised, they ultimately
expose one's experience of group interaction *as a social lesbian*. The
answers may be found by indicating to what extent one's experience is
either more private and less open or more open and less private within
the 'confines' of the ghetto and within the field of potential lesbian
'political' practice, for both groups. The final test, however, will be to
determine the levels of emergence — outness to closetedness — which
each group displays in society on the whole. Recall that one of the
most important features of social lesbianism is its direct link to the
oppressive elements which determine society. If its closet doors are
swung open wide, social lesbianism has the potential to disrupt these
elements.

From the findings in Table 4.4, we see that the majority of both
groups, 75 per cent and 93 per cent, interact regularly all, most or some

of the time with other lesbians. The sick but not sorry type shows a more private and less public lesbian life-style, while the sorry but not sick type demonstrates the opposite features of social lesbianism. These conflicts within the total social lesbian experience reflect differences which exist in activating a 'sub-culture' or ghetto with other lesbians and which create inner tensions among members of the group. However, as I implied earlier, these divisions are never absolute nor totally visible. Also lesbians develop more 'social views' of themselves than those which they held previously. In effect, an open life-style becomes available to them. This transition can also be seen to affect one's relationship to society at large. In other words, increased interaction with other lesbians may propel one to make statements about one's life in a clearly public manner. Some lesbians describe this process as well as the difficulties associated with it. Although somewhat out, these lesbians experience the tensions between being ghettoized through lesbianism and being out in society, through straight friends:

'At the moment, I'm with lesbians all of the time – not that this is always very good. It's morning noon and night – with the magazine, through the office and through meetings. But, sometimes this is not a choosing that is because we've suddenly exploded as a London organization – as a kind of functioning project. I'm very aware of this. I took to the streets much more. That means meeting with other groups and other areas plus the fact that I'm very starved for culture. You know this is changing. It is a very sterile form of existence to be totally concerned with lesbians.'

Table 4.4   *Social interaction as social lesbians*

QUESTION: How often do you interact with other lesbians?

	Sick No.	%		Sorry No.	%	
All of the time	6	6		26	25.7	
Most of the time	22	22	75	39	38.6	93
Some of the time	47	47		29	28.7	
Hardly at all	24	24		6	5.9	
NA	1	1		1	1.0	
Total	100	100		101	100.0	

'All of the time I'm with lesbians, but I have heterosexual friends
and I don't intend to be with lesbians all of the time. In a way, it
could be a mistake to see lesbians all of the time because then you
get into a ghetto type of thing. So I don't want to. I obviously
am happiest with both.'

Increased ghetto interaction may have an opposite effect in total
separatism. Separatism is a lesbian way of life, usually more for the
sorry but not sick type than for the sick but not sorry type, based upon
the idea that one should relate only to women who are lesbian-orientated
or at least much more open to women than to men. Therefore, for
some the ghetto experience becomes a total way of life. Men are
excluded from the field of relationships. When asked, 'How often are
you with other lesbians', separatists said the following:

'I'm with lesbians every day in living with them, at discos, odd
gatherings that go on here and there. Well, I think every day my
whole life is tied up with dykes, every 2 minutes.'

'24 hours a day (laugh).'

'Actually, all of the time.'

It is also interesting to look at the levels of outness and closetedness
which vary between the two types of lesbians (Table 4.5). Although

Table 4.5   *The levels of outness and closetedness for social lesbians*

		Sick No.	%		Sorry No.	%	
Out	1	34	34	75% tendency to be out	59	58.8	98.2% tendency to be out
	2	9	9		15	14.8	
	3	14	14		11	10.8	
	4	18	18		14	13.8	
	5	1	1	25% tendency to be in closet	0		1.8% tendency to be in closet
	6	17	17		2	1.8	
	7	0			0		
Closet	8	7	7		0		

75 per cent of the sick but not sorry type have a tendency to be out,
the group as a whole displays a higher proportion in the closet than the

sorry but not sick type, 25 per cent as opposed to 1.8 per cent respectively, and 98 per cent of the latter group have a tendency to be out. These findings appear to be consistent with my previous findings. If one group of social lesbians accepts a somewhat private view of sexuality (as, by definition, the sick but not sorry type appear to do), they will most likely show a higher proportion of closetedness than the group which tends to uphold a public notion of sexuality (i.e. sorry but not sick type). Although the majority of both types have a tendency to be out, the sorry but not sick type maintains a larger majority. I would contend that one of the essential elements of social lesbianism is the implicit resistance to society's view that sexuality is private. Yet, in the midst of this resistance or opposition, repressive features are present. And, we see that some who glorify the past also hang on to traditional views of sexuality. These lesbians are fearful of change as well as afraid of being out of the closet. However, this is not always true. One 'out' lesbian, while accepting society's views of 'sex as private' as well as 'lesbians as sick', demonstrates the existing conflicts within the lesbian phenomenon. In a contradictory sense, she upholds traditional views which are related to her social position, but she rejects the social imperative to be secretive, private or, simply, in the closet. The theory is upheld, while the practice is not:

'I probably came out earlier than most which was unusual because of my age group [this lesbian is 55 years old]. I always wanted people to understand me because let's face it everybody wants to be liked and I've never been ostracized in any way. At the slightest opportunity while I've never pushed it on anybody, with any suggestion, I've always said, "Well, yes, I am a lesbian". I've done that kind of thing from quite early on – from coming out of the army . . . . Well, you know there is a thing that it's got to be a give and a take thing and not to get all up in arms about.'

Stakes within a male-orientated system

As women, lesbians are ultimately determined by their position within a patriarchal capitalist order. Be that as it may, they live in a man's world. However, their awareness of a male-dominated society and of their dependence upon it varies as do their stakes within it. Many social lesbians become conscious of sexism. They are aware of those disruptive forces which create the alienation and isolation of women as well as women's 'vocation' to be dependent upon men. Some lesbians realize that they challenge these social realities:

'For me, lesbianism is a total way of life but it can't be total in terms of how society sees it . . . I mean you're affected by society, by a sexist society so it can't actually be total. It's tied up with you as an individual and how you relate. Is it a male way or isn't it?'

'It's a conscious policy that women are kept isolated. A perfect example is of women and how they are subjected to things in hospital, alienated from their bodies. One gyny [gynaecologist] told us that 50 per cent of births end up in caesarean sections because male technology is too feeble to discover foetal irregularity. It's a most amazing kind of alienation of women's basic function. I don't particularly want to have a child at this point in time. To think that men decide how a woman is going to have a baby in that kind of arbitrary fashion is horrifying to me. It's a horrible way that men keep women isolated from one another and their basic function.'

'The whole thing that women are meant to feel unattractive because they have hairy legs or are fat, etc. is a way that men through conditioning (which is all for money or their own wanking egos) keep women apart from each other. If one woman is prettier than the other, the other gets jealous. I found the more that I thought about it this is exactly how a male system works. If women can see what's being done to them, then men haven't got a chance.'

'All we have is women. It knocks you out when you realize that is all you've got. It's nice to have a coloured telly. It's nice to have a stereo, but hell, that's nothing and that's what male society is — coloured televisions, Rolls Royces, bloody Concordes and all we've got is ourselves which is what life is all about.'

Regardless of how critical of 'male society' lesbians remain, they are, nevertheless, dependent upon male society for the satisfaction of their basic material needs, i.e. money, food, clothing, shelter, etc. While they are a 'deviant group' and objectively criticize society or social norms, they, in some way, must get support from this system.

Yet, how much support, whether through work or ideas, do they give to this self-same system?

Lesbians' stakes within the system are measurable by the extent to which their support of society takes priority, explicitly or implicitly, over and above their criticisms of society. Often, their material position as women, and ultimate dependence upon a patriarchal capitalist society, effectively tones down their potential as social lesbians to challenge society as well as to resist its dominance over their lives. In effect, they may loose some of their potential for struggle as an oppressed group. Many lesbians, like many women, find it necessary

Table 4.6   *Occupations of social lesbians*

	Sick No.	%		Sorry No.	%	
Professional or higher managerial (Company directors, high level managers, etc.)	6	6		3	3.0	
Professional or lower managerial (Administrators, doctors, lawyers, university teachers, etc.)	15	15	59%	11	10.9	38.7%
Supervisory or skilled (Nursing supervisors, lecturers in higher education, higher levels in civil service)	38	38		25	24.8	
Lower non-manual (Nurses, teachers, low levels in the civil service)	17	17		12	11.9	
Skilled manual (Clerical workers, secretaries)	8	8		10	9.9	
Unskilled manual (Agricultural workers, factory and domestic workers)	7	7		5	5.0	
Residual, state pensioners	1	1		–	–	
Students	4	4		16	15.8	
Unemployed	2	2		9	8.9	
NA	2	2		10	9.9	
Total	100	100		101	100.0	

to work for a wage outside the immediate family context. While lesbians have a tendency to be free from the husband-marriage-children-family syndrome as well as from a husband's wage and domestic labour, many lesbians are dependent upon *themselves* for subsistence. In other words, their wages are *essential* for their survival. We see that lesbians in this sample are engaged in a variety of occupations (Table 4.6).

In the light of the figures in Table 4.6, it is interesting to note that a higher percentage of sick (59 per cent) than sorry (38.7 per cent) were distributed in the three highest occupational levels. One explanation of this tendency, which is consistent with my previous findings, could be that the sick but not sorry type has more of a stake within the system than the sorry but not sick type. The former group upholds convention. In other words, their career goals and occupational commitments reflect not only the wider society's expectations for them as career-orientated women,[3] but also their social origins and interests as being predominantly middle-class. For them, the privileges which are linked to occupational status, career advancement and possible upward social mobility for women outweigh the 'choice' of a certain level of what is in society's eyes social or material deprivation. This latter choice is the ultimate implication for an ideological orientation. What I am attempting to point out here are the primary, vested interests of each group of social lesbians. Within the context of the lesbian struggle, the 'more conventional' lesbians, although in a socially 'deviant' group, do not appear to jeopardize their material advantages or social position as women. Simply, they stake more claims within the system than the more ideologically orientated type. As a group, they show a vested interest not only in traditional views of lesbianism but also in the perpetuation of social convention. Notwithstanding their 'progressive' social orientation, the tradition-bound social lesbians stifle the group's political potential as well as lessen the social lesbian critique of society.

On the other hand, although 38 per cent of the sorry but not sick type appear within the three highest occupational levels, they tend to contain the most radical type of social lesbian or those who are ideologically orientated. I have observed within this latter group a disdain for any form of career commitment or long-term occupational goal. The justification for this distance from material advancement is that any form of employment ultimately services an oppressive society (patriarchal and/or capitalist). Therefore, some support the view that it is impossible to engage in 'meaningful employment'. (Perhaps a majority of the unemployed express these sentiments.) As a result, some lesbians remain unemployed and actively refuse to take part in a labour force which they feel not only oppresses workers but also oppresses women as a secondary workforce.

In a similar ideological framework, but with different material implications, there are those who are highly educated and objectively career-orientated. On a conscious level, they reject any previous occupational goals and employment practices which imply upward social mobility. In effect, they re-orientate their total work ethic and redirect their career prospects to lower occupational levels. The implication is that some lesbians will re-train in a variety of 'male-defined' occupations, such as electricians, car mechanics, plumbers or carpenters. Through their newly acquired skills, they attempt to challenge society's views towards certain áreas of skilled manual labour which have traditionally been male-dominated. These lesbians explore the contradictions which they feel are inherent in a system which exploits the female worker. Also, they prove that women are capable of going beyond their 'expected' work-role (i.e. as secretaries, nurses, teachers, etc.) and that women can do 'men's jobs'.

Another area in which tradition holds a firm grasp and which may reveal a certain number of stakes within the system is religion (see Table 4.7).

Table 4.7   *Social lesbians and religion*

	Sick No.	%		Sorry No.	%	
Church of England	20	20	⎫	5	5.0	⎫
Catholic	9	9	⎪	5	5.0	⎪
Jewish	2	2	⎪	2	2.0	⎪
Quaker	1	1	⎪	1	1.0	⎪
Christian	3	3	⎬ 46%	5	5.0	⎬ 23%
Buddhist	2	2	⎪	3	3.0	⎪
Methodist	4	4	⎪	2	2.0	⎭
Spiritualist	2	2	⎪	–	–	
Other	3	3	⎭	–	–	
NA	54	54		78	77.0	
Total	100	100		101	100.0	

As far as religion is concerned, the majority of social lesbians (65 per cent of 201) and the majority in both groups (54 per cent and 77 per cent did not view themselves as having any current religious affiliation, regardless of any previous affiliation. However, 46 per cent of the sick but not sorry type as opposed to 23 per cent of the sorry but not sick type maintain a religious orientation. These findings concerning religious affiliation do not contradict the previous findings in this chapter. In other words, we see again the tension which exists between tradition and politics for social lesbians. On the one hand, the sick but not sorry type reveal a tendency towards tradition through their employment practice, ideas about themselves, their views of change, and their religious affiliation. On the other hand, the sorry but not sick type shift towards ideology through innovative ideas about themselves and social change, by questioning and possibly rejecting traditional spirituality or religion, and by developing a potential 'political' base for lesbians.

Within the context of this potential for political struggle, the following chapter will outline the implications of these tendencies for the development of lesbian consciousness, the differences and similarities between social lesbians' criticisms of society and the ways in which these tendencies and criticisms merge into practice.

5 Lesbian consciousness and lesbian practice

Previously we saw that three stages of consciousness had emerged from the lesbian struggle. They were the apolitical, the pre-political and the political. Historically, these stages reflect lesbianism as a traditional form, a social form and an ideological form, respectively. Furthermore, it is important to remember that all forms of lesbianism are present in society in varying degrees and levels of consciousness. However, today, it appears that the most predominant form is social lesbianism. With this development, two types of lesbians become visible. While each type emphasizes a particular tendency, both types together become united in a struggle against society. In general, this struggle is characterized by a desire for social change. In particular, these desires build up either as a reaction against social norms or as an attack against society's structure and, ultimately, its continuance.

On the one hand, social lesbians with traditional tendencies (sick) desire social tolerance. Gradually, their desires are transformed into demands. Through these demands, they attempt to alter social attitudes towards lesbians. On the other hand, those with ideological tendencies (sorry) insist upon change through resistance. They attack not only social attitudes but also the root cause of these attitudes: society's structure. Through this latter position, social lesbians resist the structure of sexual relationships and the struggle for power. In effect, they attempt to root out all forms of sexual oppression and/or social oppression.

The basis of each type's demands and attempts at social change varies in terms of their awareness of lesbian oppression. However, both types merge in their experience of being women. Each group's involvement in lesbian practice is determined not only by group activity but by group consciousness. Albeit both have similar levels of awareness, each group expresses it more in line with a particular orientation than not. Within the total social lesbian experience, both types are critical, but each in their own way. However, let us not forget that each type is neither static nor unbending as it moves through society. Furthermore, both groups not only appear to oppose each other but also appear together as a distinct lesbian form — social lesbianism. Therefore, rather than extreme polarities in a single force, imagine a spectrum of shifting elements which conflict with each other but which have a tendency to minimize conflict by a forward movement.

Desire for tolerance vs challenge through resistance

A pre-political consciousness implies that social lesbians have the potential to threaten society or, at least, to challenge traditional views of lesbianism.

The attitudes of the sick but not sorry type reveal a general movement forward among social lesbians. This ideological shift exposes a certain unwillingness to accept conventional social beliefs about themselves. Because of the support which they receive from the group context, they are able to progress as social lesbians and to develop their quest for social tolerance. Their modest hope is for social acceptance rather than any form of radical social change.

> 'Tolerant, tolerant, tolerant . . . . Society must be. I've got no
> hangups against any other human being. They sort out their lives
> and I sort out mine. If society expects me to be tolerant of its ways,
> people's feelings or it's attitudes, society must reciprocate and
> accept me.'

> 'People should be tolerant of homosexuals. For example, my father
> is. In fact, he had a row with my sister because she called someone
> a puff. My father said, "Do you know what that means?" "No, not
> really," she said. He really laid into her. I said, "Wow, this is really
> fantastic because you're obviously really tolerant of it all." He's
> more than tolerant. He actually accepts it and teaches his children
> not to ridicule it. More people should be like him.'

It is interesting to note that this desire for tolerance emphasizes society's acceptance of an individual as well as focusing on the personal aspect or subjective experience of lesbianism. Again, but in a different context, the power of tradition surfaces. It compels those who do not fit into socially acceptable roles to 'individualize' their experiences. However, by the very fact that these lesbians emerge from a group context and a specific lesbian awareness, they gradually wear down their links with the past. Developing as social critics, they become better able to challenge tradition.

Other social lesbians may emphasize the more progressive tendencies of social lesbianism. Shifting towards political consciousness, they begin to question the organization of social life and the total structure of society. By going to the 'root' of the problem (society's structure), they reveal the radical aspects of lesbian consciousness. As ideologically directed, they accumulate 'fuel for the fire' or 'weapons for the attack'. They launch a campaign against the 'nature' of society. In support of their position, they level criticisms against the view that 'all women should be emotionally dependent upon men'. For them, as for others, lesbianism not only objectively but subjectively rejects this idea:

'It is not emotional dependence upon men. I don't know whether it makes it better and easier or not, but I suppose in some ways it makes it easier on the whole, given that on the whole men are pretty lousy to get along with.'

'For most women, a women's life is intertwined with a guy's and totally dependent upon him. I could be classified as different in that sort of set-up. It comes down to society's views of women as producers of children.'

In a similar critical vein, others challenge women's traditional identity as being 'naturally' male-defined or 'inherently' family-orientated:

'Women don't have a personality of their own. Every action they make or the way they look is to appeal to men, to get a husband, to have children. That's what it is all about – all brainwashing. You know, bit by bit.'

'Women provide for their families. I suppose to a certain extent it is true that most of them are able to talk about the price of fish or baby clothes and things like that . . . . If you get two housewives together, they'll talk about these things because it's the only thing that they have in common. Housewives are made to identify with food and clothes. They've been denied everything else by their assumed role they had to take on. Well, people need their identity and for us, when it's taken away, we have to create one out of what we have. If you're a housewife, there is not much of an identity as I see it.'

Extending these comments, some lesbians question the 'naturalness' of woman's child-bearing role as a mother. In this way they criticize society's view that all women should not only be mothers but also want to be mothers:

'Once, my teacher talked about childbirth. He says that I have extremist views. I told him that I don't want children. He said, "You must want children; it's natural." I said, "If I don't want it, it's not natural." I said, "If I have a child because I'm told to then it's not natural. I don't want to have one." He comes back with, "Yes, but you're biologically built. You have a womb, etc." It got really very heavy. That was sick. I mean he thought that every woman wants to have a child and to look after children and to stay at home and to look after the family. For him, he stated categorically, "A woman's place is in the home." My English lectures are battlefields. You can imagine.'

Because social lesbians tend to have a critical stance in relationship to women's position in society, they appear to reject the importance of family life for women:

'Lesbianism is very different in terms of a lesbian's identification with the family. I mean usually the family takes priority in terms of one's own family, husband or children. They are one's vital links. Our vital links to society have not much to do with the family. This means that our priorities as servicing or being parental are not made.'

As women, lesbians neither establish their expected 'vital links' with society nor, therefore, respond in a way which is consistent for 'acceptable women'. As a result, their social reaction or criticisms of society tend to expose their position in relationship to the dominant ideology. This ideology proposes that lesbians 'want to be men' or are 'unfeminine'. Society responds negatively to the lesbian image and lesbians are aware of this:

'In many ways, society reacts negatively. It reacts in terms of a bunch
of freaky women who are analysed in terms of male-copying or
male-emulating women. Lesbianism is basically invalidated by
society. It's not given any credence by society. It's explained away
as either freakish or mannish, I mean it's not seen as a female way of
behaving. It's anti- the feminine role. It's anti-feminine.'

Because they deny women's traditional role as well as the conventional role for lesbians, these lesbians develop a unique social perspective and view of their lives. Although they reflect 'living inconsistencies'
of what society expects for women and lesbians, they manifest two
important, if not crucial, elements in the total lesbian struggle. First,
lesbianism is more than a sexual preference, and second, lesbianism is
directly related to women's position in an oppressive society. As a
potential social force, lesbians are combatants against a society which
is determined by competition for sexual favours as well as money.
Lesbianism challenges power; it affects many areas of social life.

'The moral of the story — "Once you're known as a lesbian, it taints
everything else." It taints anything that you might say on a political
matter, yet you're tainted by the fact that you sleep with women.
The fact that you may have extreme views on women's position in
society is immaterial to people who have the power within it. They
can't see the importance of these issues on their own because all they
see is that you sleep with women and they don't like it.'

'Well, lesbianism is not competitive. That's the thing. It really
freaked me out when I had to compete with men on a newspaper
that I was working on. I was a second-class citizen, basically. If I
had to get on, I had to be like the men and I couldn't be like that
even if I wanted to. I realize that that's not the way to do it. Now,
I still have lots of competitive instincts but again that's part of the
old life. I still have to change. We aren't competitive and we have
fights among women. It's not sweetness and light — but it's not
competitive.'

From the above, we see that by developing a type of 'radical critique'
of society, some social lesbians experience an awareness of their oppression. This awareness, in turn, enables them to build up pockets of resistance which challenges society's ill-treatment of them. The dominant

ideology is exposed. This particular group of lesbians acts as a catalyst for change not only within a wide social context but also within the narrow confines of the lesbian ghetto. In the latter area, they appear to question traditional tendencies of particular social lesbians as well as to contradict the ghetto's emphasis upon the isolation of lesbianism as a social phenomenon. In effect, the more ideologically orientated among them have the potential to wear away the elements of isolation and tradition and thus to thrust a critique of lesbianism into the mainstream of social life.

Women's struggle and lesbianism: convergence, consensus and contradiction

When viewing their position as lesbians in light of the general oppression and subordination of all women in society, both types of social lesbians appear to express similar concerns. It seems that when they consider the relationship between lesbianism and women, social lesbians blend their ideas together harmoniously. It is this consideration which causes them to come very close to striking a single, yet resounding, note in society. Perhaps their prelude to political consciousness and group struggle compels them to search for common grounds with women and to establish the vital links between lesbian consciousness and the consciousness of all women. Perhaps their struggle necessitates the convergence of these two forms of consciousness, which are, apparently, distinct in society's eyes.

From my observation of this process, I would contend that, as a group, social lesbians faintly reflect this convergence. Furthermore, with future development, they have the potential to alter social consciousness or to help society to grow. Regardless of this potential, what are the implications of this somewhat apparent consensus among social lesbians? How do they express this consensus? Also, to what extent do they as a group establish links between their consciousness as lesbians and their consciousness as women? Or, what characterizes the consciousness of social lesbians?

Chapter 3 discussed social lesbians' deepening awareness as women in society. Therefore, the group's experience of this awareness becomes acutely felt, as members consistently struggle against women's subordination. While they confront oppression in all areas of their social lives, they express consensus as social lesbians. Consciously or unconsciously, they solidify the bonds between themselves and women. Nevertheless, aware of their contradictory position as lesbian/women, they attempt to bridge the gap which society has created between lesbians, who are women, and women, who are oppressed in a male-dominated society. Some lesbians expressed their concern over these issues in the following ways:

'Lesbians and women are not at all contradictory except in society's eyes and views. Lesbian is a woman, who is a lesbian. That's why the word, lesbian, is better than female homosexual. In society's eyes, woman is female, male-identified and in love with men. Lesbian is the opposite. But, not in my terms.'

'Well, to quote from another lesbian . . . . What is the phrase? . . . "She can't be a woman, she must be a dyke." The two are contradictory as society sees it and cannot be together. If you're a dyke, then you cannot be a woman. You're only pretending to be a man. But, on the personal level, the two are very intertwined and they have to be. To be a lesbian, I have to be a woman.'

'If society is going to accept us, it has to accept us as we are and not according to their conception which is really a male phallic concept of women.'

'Lesbians – what could be more counter to the male identity or the male-structured society? I don't think we've found out yet what a women's identity is, but we're groping towards it. I think lesbians will do a hell of a lot. We must be included as women.'

'Our lives are so interwoven with the needs of women and the status of women too.'

'Lesbianism is still an emotive word. It doesn't yet mean or describe to society what it is to be a woman and a woman-identified woman and a woman loving woman and being loved by woman. Because, it filters right out into the thing that women should get passionately upset about – battered mums, lesbians having their children taken away from them (which as a childless lesbian doesn't have to hassle me) . . . . But, it all hassles me as a woman. It makes me mad when issues like abortion come up. I burn all over as a woman because someone is dictating the function of my body and the bodies of women that I love and care about.'

'The lesbian is woman. I'm thinking more and more that I'm less and less a lesbian and more and more a woman. I find them so closely interrelated whereas before I thought being a lesbian was a total separate thing.'

'I still don't think there is any difference in how we as lesbians feel than the heterosexual woman. I mean why shouldn't women's rights apply to all of us. It's not just for one section of us.'

Although lesbians are viewed by society, as well as by some women, as being removed from the social group 'women', they struggle none the less, to maintain an important, if not integral position in the movement towards women's liberation. During this transition period, they appear to join together with other oppressed women, even if these women are also lesbians. Knowingly or unknowingly, they not only make clear the lesbian situation *vis à vis* women's but also strengthen the lesbian challenge to their subservient position, in relationship either to men or other women. In this way, they also establish bonds with all women who combat power.

It appears that social lesbians, to a limited extent, search for and uncover hidden connections between their consciousness as lesbians and as women. Yet, their response is limited according to the development of their 'lesbian' consciousness. Emerging with an understanding of their past and a clearer vision of its impact on the present, they grow and develop. However, most social lesbians have not yet made visible a political consciousness for lesbians. By denying the connections between lesbianism and feminism, some hold back the group's potential to become politically conscious and to create blueprints for the future. In effect, they seem to stifle the development of lesbianism as an ideological form. This form establishes lesbianism in a political context. Lesbianism becomes closely bound up within women's total struggle. In other words, the links between lesbianism and feminism are firmly established. (These implications will be discussed in more detail in the following chapter.)

All the same, through social lesbianism, many become increasingly aware of the crucial relationship between women's experience and the lesbian experience. Lesbians begin to grow in their knowledge of a collective history which they share with women. Yet, as we have seen, many will not accept a close relationship between lesbianism and feminism. Although the majority maintain that only a vague connection exists between the two 'women's issues', they continually expand their ideas. Discouraged by the past and society's treatment of them, they create a social problem. The next step would imply a transition from their group consciousness as lesbians to a developing consciousness with all women. In this way, they help to create an ideological context in which the issues of lesbianism and feminism become closely knit.

The creation of lesbian political consciousness with other women enables them not only to gather strength as a social force but also to initiate the process which wears down society's rigidity as well as women's traditional position within this rigid structure. Social lesbianism makes visible these in-built possibilities and tensions.

A pivotal point of agreement is the awareness of being women. (Remember that 75 per cent saw themselves as being closely linked up to women, while 83 per cent revealed a high level of 'women-commitment'.) However, regardless of this consensus, they upheld a variety of opinions concerning the 'lesbian issue' as it relates to the 'women issue' or feminism. Less than half established a close relationship between the two. Often consensus implied contradiction. Within this apparently similar group, tensions emerge. Seemingly, lesbians are not yet aware of their impact upon society or of their collective history as an oppressed group. In spite of this, some uphold the relevance of feminism for their development and appear to manifest this awareness. In this way, they shift towards ideology and help to form political consciousness:

'I can see that being a lesbian may mean that one might not necessarily be a feminist but for me being a lesbian does involve being a feminist of sorts.'

'Feminism is a word that I never really know what it means. I mean it's to do with women. Right. And, I am a woman.'

Other lesbians with this awareness envisioned the disruptive elements which they felt lesbianism could bring upon feminism:

'Whether it should be or not, lesbianism can be a real wedge. It's because once you've taken that step, what does a man become? He becomes a sex machine. Who needs him when sex is not just fucking? It's the whole relating thing for women. It's the emotional experience.'

'I never knew what feminism was. I thought it was probably something pretty with curls. But lesbianism for me now is tied up with feminism. It doesn't have to be so because there are many lesbians who have no feminist consciousness or awareness, but are lesbians. It's not an integral part of it for them. Would that it were, it would make the whole thing erupt.'

Also, there are those who deny the social or historical implications which feminism has for the development and emergence of lesbianism. Although these lesbians appear to accept the fact that lesbianism has evolved in history, they do not establish all of their crucial links with the past. Their historical perspective remains incomplete. However, these same lesbians predispose themselves to a clearer vision and to becoming fully aware of important connections (and necessary relationships). They have the potential to become conscious as lesbians. Therefore, all is not lost; their potential for 'politics' carries them along, while they reveal a critical stance in society. Yet, sometimes, this group separates themselves from other women. This separation thwarts a full consciousness or political growth. Furthermore, a division is effected between lesbianism and feminism. Lesbians cut off their history from women's history. This explains why some lesbians question the development of 'lesbian politics' with a feminist framework:

'No, they aren't related. I don't see them in these terms.'

'People who are lesbians are not feminists but feminists should be sympathetic to lesbians.'

'I can see the two are separate things. I don't see the two together. Some of the greatest feminists I know are straight.'

One lesbian who said that she was neither 'a political animal' nor 'a feminist' appears to contradict not only the above statements but also herself.

'I would say lesbianism and feminism are linked. I would think all lesbians are feminists but all feminists aren't lesbians. I would say

that being a lesbian is sort of a positive thing because you're not
tied up with a man you know. You pay your own bills get your
own food and you are in the position of being an independent
women. There you are a single autonomous female. You haven't
got kids – that terrible tie which could be a disadvantage. There
are lesbians who have children but a great many don't.'

Whether or not society upholds this view, lesbians see themselves as
women. But, because society has consistently attempted to separate
lesbians from women, lesbians themselves have become confused.
Historically, they may or may not know where they came from, while
politically they may or may not understand where they are going.
Difficulties arise because they have been removed from a major part of
their history by society as well as by themselves. Where is their development as women with women? In a variety of ways, history has worked
against lesbians. But, luckily, many are becoming aware of this fact.
Conscious of their history and of their absence in society, lesbians
attempt to compensate for their isolation or to make up for this lack.
Many are finding it more and more fruitful to challenge their invisibility.
Not surprisingly, they place more emphasis upon themselves as lesbians
than as women. However, in their struggle to re-emerge from history,
they often set up barriers which make it difficult for them to retain
links with the past or their total history as women. As a result, lesbian
chauvinism emerges and lesbians begin to espouse the belief that the
lesbian way of life is either 'the best way of life for a woman' or 'the
only way of life for women'.

'Lesbianism is feminism.'

'I shall offer you on this occasion an historical quotation from
Ti-Grace-Atkinson. "Feminism is the theory of which lesbianism
is the practice." '

'Feminism is the theory, lesbianism is the practice. Again, I really
don't disassociate the two. Just by living your life-style – being
who you are, you don't have to go proselytizing. You just walk
down the street.'

'Lesbianism is the ultimate for feminism. To be totally chauvinistic
– feminism means a total rejection of our society. One of the best

ways to reject our male-orientated society is to be lucky enough
to be a lesbian. As far as I'm concerned, all lesbians should be
feminists and hopefully, all feminists should be lesbians.'

These beliefs include, whether explicitly or not, the idea that feminism is in some way equated with lesbianism and vice versa. On the one
hand, lesbians attempt to collapse the division between the two ways of
life for women. On the other hand, by upholding a distinctly 'chauvinist'
position, they separate themselves from the feminist struggle and in the
last analysis from women. They forget their history.

Here we see emerging the tensions and contradictions which lesbians
experience in their demand for recognition. Applying their knowledge
of the past to the present, they appear to separate sexuality from
society. While emphasizing a traditional sexual orientation for women,
they divorce themselves from their self-definition as women. Becoming
more aware of their individual and subsequent group choices, they
make fleeting attempts to understand the implications of their alternatives. While removing their personal situation from a political framework in feminism, they attract notice to the individual solution of a
social problem (lesbianism). In other words, lesbian chauvinists create
more divisions in the already existing contradictions between sexuality
and society; lesbians and women; lesbianism and feminism and the
personal and the political.

Perhaps, the following comments come closest to illustrating the
general tone of the ideas which they express and the broad direction
towards which social lesbians progress:

'Lesbianism and feminism are not necessarily related, but obviously,
they become related. Perhaps, we feel things more strongly than
a heterosexual feminist. But, I don't know one way or the other.
What about the man in her life? But, I suppose what I said about
us feeling more strongly isn't true because feminism is pro-men
anyways as well as pro-women. What I think it's trying to achieve
is a more balanced life for everybody. At this point, anyways, men
carry most of the responsibility like being money earners and
working and running the world. An enormous amount probably
want to share their responsibility with women. I always argue this
point very strongly because it's so obvious inequalities exist and
that we live in a man's world. But sometimes, I've misread whether
because I'm a lesbian or a believer in feminism I don't know.'

Lesbian practice – apolitical, pre-political or political?

In modern parlance, practice refers to 'habitual performance of an act' or 'to carry out in action'. Practice implies theory or a particular way of looking at society, a problem, others or oneself. To be practical indicates that one thinks about what one does and vice versa. Practice also means that there should be a certain level of consistency between the two – what one thinks and what one does. Often, however, in everyday society theory contradicts practice and practice opposes theory.

For lesbians, practice becomes an area which is clouded over in history by layers of isolation and fear. It has been difficult for lesbians not only to get beneath the layers but also to explain why they are still there, or even there! As we have seen, particular views had emerged from this struggle and society created explanations for the lesbian. Yet, for some, and now, possibly, for many, these explanations were not consistent with how one lived one's life. More simply, theories about lesbianism contradicted what lesbians actually feel and do about themselves. Social lesbians who have reached this stage of development question what they have been told by society:

'Lesbianism affects one's attitude towards society and to everyone in society. If a lesbian is aware that what society has told us about itself and women is lies, then it affects one's whole way of looking at politics, economics, etc. One has a lesbian perspective on everything – like the way we govern.'

It will not be easy to describe the different types of lesbian practice which have evolved and which are still evolving. In spite of the divisions in practice between both types of social lesbians, I will look at how lesbian practice has emerged from specific types of lesbian consciousness for all social lesbians. I have described not only social lesbians' predominant characterization by a pre-political consciousness but also how and why they tend to manifest this type of awareness. Also, I have described the various tendencies, whether towards ideology or tradition, which exist within social lesbianism. However, imagine that the above somewhat static, descriptive account is in reality a dynamic process – pregnant with conflict and contradiction as well as apparent harmony and bliss. The process of lesbian emergence links up as well as makes divisions between and among society and lesbians; lesbians and women; lesbians and lesbians, and lesbian and lesbian.

The process is reminiscent of particles of energy or atoms. While dividing within themselves, they gather momentum and force through space. In space, power or molecular force grows as they conflict with one another. Opposite energy fields are created. Yet, ultimately, 'supreme' power is achieved when chance collision collapses the divisions between poles. Unity exists. (However, if manipulated in a particular way, i.e., through nuclear power, energy has the potential to be a destructive force through space.)

Social lesbian practice[1] is a complex changing process. Despite the difficulties of analysis, it can be roughly classified as follows: straight lesbians, status quo lesbians, reformist or liberal lesbians and 'fringe' or marginal lesbians.

Straight lesbians – collusion

Those who look to the 'straight' or 'heterosexual' world for models of how they should live and be lesbian are straight lesbians. They tend to cling to traditional lesbian images and uphold the butch (masculine) and femme (feminine) roles. Having a low level of awareness, they desire to conceal from society their lesbian orientation. They usually isolate themselves within the closet. Consistent with tradition and an apolitical consciousness, they have a tendency to accept definitions of lesbianism as 'sick' or 'socially deficient'. This would account for why they go to great lengths to hide their lesbianism. Lesbianism is a 'state', an in-built characteristic or a sexual preference. It is not a choice for them. As born lesbians, they eliminate this element on any level. Most do not question why lesbians exist. They merely accept it as a fact of life. In effect, straight lesbians offer no challenge to social norms but simply collude with society's definitions. Self-images are defined solely in sexual terms – 'I am a woman who has sex with other women.' These images help to carry along the traditional focus which society has created. Although there is not any comparable focus on sex in the straight world, these lesbians perpetuate this focus upon and for themselves. Social acceptability implies not only the 'assumption' of heterosexual roles for lesbians but also the presumption that straight lesbians are indeed 'straight' and therefore defined by a social given: all people in society are straight.

Straight lesbians are as important to the lesbian struggle as sexism is to the general struggle against women's oppression. Neither struggle is given consideration. As non-critics, they perpetuate the traditional form of lesbianism. Their only concern is for a veneer of respectability mingled with the unquestioning desire for approval and acceptance on society's terms.

Status quo lesbians – conformism?

Like the above type, status quo lesbians do not want to accentuate lesbianism in society. As primarily closeted, they have little if any political potential. However, unlike the straight lesbians, they tend to reject the utility or necessity of imitating the straight world. While embodying some of the characteristics of social lesbians in an awareness of group context, they maintain many stakes within the system, for example the desire for social acceptability. Perhaps, this particular excerpt from Abbott and Love best describes their specific practice:

> Some lesbians in the straight world strive to appear to be asexual, non-descript or even neuter. They do not want to look too feminine which would put psychological restrictions on behavior and attract attention from men and they do not want to look too masculine which seems equally unnatural. The point is, a lesbian is not an excessively sexual creature, as she is expected to be. But, if she is indeed a total person with sex an integrated part of her life, some may find this bizarre.[2]

Abbott and Love see that while tending to remain non-descript, the status quo lesbians reject a total, sexual definition of lesbianism. In a sense, while being politically unaware, they manifest a predisposition to this type of awareness. By rejecting some of society's traditional views, status quo lesbians consider themselves 'normal people' or 'average lesbians', as some say. Whether they feel that they are born lesbians or self-chosen lesbians, they experience an expanding view of their position. They may be somewhat out of the ordinary in society's eyes. But, regardless of that fact, they feel that they are able to manage. Basically, they go along with the mundane existence of life – family, job, friends, etc. – like the average, single, heterosexual woman. On an individual level, lesbianism becomes an integrated part of their lives. Yet, they do not want to upset the conformist stance of their lives by becoming more involved in the lesbian ghetto than they actually are. An awareness of the lesbian struggle is not important. What remains primary is the need to conform to society's images of, if not outward expectations for, a normal woman. For them, lesbianism is a commitment to women but not a total way of life within the context of a struggle. Status quo lesbians lead what any unknowing bystander would term normal lives.

Reformist lesbians and pressure groups

Objectively, these lesbians appear as potentially political. They maintain a somewhat critical position in society. By challenging traditional views of lesbianism, they attempt to bring about some type of change within society for lesbians. While accepting the basic structure of society as well as the traditional organization of power, they endeavour to change a part, not all, of the existing order. Reformist lesbians become involved in criticizing the existing social norms which put down 'gays' and/or 'women' as 'minority groups'. As a result, they form visible groups which react to these social norms; which exert pressure upon society and which point out certain defects in the ideals of equality, liberalism or individualism in western society. 'Gay rights' or 'women's rights' are their slogans and they utilize existing social institutions (educational system, religion, legal system, and political system) as their platforms for recognition. Ultimately, reformist lesbians do not challenge society at its core. In society's eye, this type of pressure group acts as a splinter which can, in the long run, be taken out or accommodated within the total system. This splinter remains unseen as well as fitting into a very limited and well controlled area. Regardless of that fact, reformist lesbians tend to be out and quite involved in the lesbian ghetto, which they have helped to create. Yet, they also have a tendency to become politicized. If and when, as a pressure group, they desire rapid social change, they may transform themselves into a resistance group. In other words, they expose the need for structural change and shift towards a form of resistance. In this respect, political consciousness becomes evident. Respectability is forgotten in favour of group struggle.

It is interesting to note that often lesbians become politically aware when they are discriminated against as women in predominantly male-orientated gay reformist groups, such as CHE, or as lesbians in women's reformist groups. Sometimes, in the attempt to minimize social problems and conflict on a large scale within society the pressure group maximizes conflict within itself (disagreement on group's policy). The result is that they may lose political potential as well as a certain level of group respectability, which is their ultimate aim. They may create problems in their own areas of 'pressure'. These are some of the problems which exist for reformist lesbians.

Marginal areas of lesbian practice -- lesbians on the 'fringe'

To be a bisexual, a mother or a celibate appears as a challenge not only to society's image of a lesbian but often to a lesbian's image of herself. While appearing on the fringe or as a marginal grouping in relationship to lesbian practice, the very existence of these lesbians tends to upset the acceptable notions of sexuality, motherhood and lesbianism. For example, a woman should be either heterosexual or homosexual – straight or gay (she should preferably be straight). Only real women (heterosexual) should be mothers; lesbians aren't real women. Lesbianism is about active sex; celibacy is about abstinence. These lesbians on the fringe may hold a low place or experience little 'status' within the lesbian ghetto. Other lesbians may tend to view them as not being true lesbians or as those who are not fully committed to lesbianism.

Bisexuals – the 'best of two worlds' or a 'challenge to sexuality'?
Bisexuals become visible as a threat to heterosexual women and lesbians alike. Their presence tends to bring out fears of heterosexuality in lesbians as well as fears of lesbianism for straight women. Some lesbians categorize bisexuals as 'women in transition'.[3]

Others feel that this practice is a 'cop-out' because bisexuals still define themselves in terms of men. Thus, bisexuals seem to lend support to the dominant sexual ideology. Still others contend that, as a 'positive experience', bisexuality may be the only way some women will experience women both sexually and on a deep emotional level.

Bisexuality has become an enigmatic position. It is marginal in the ghetto as well as in society. Bisexuals, lacking consciousness, become static in their quest for personal sexual liberation. They may experience a high turnover in their sexual relationships with men and women, but they question neither why they have the need nor why bisexuality exists or more importantly, why it should exist. Conscious bisexuals actively create alternatives within a sexually oppressive society which does not make room for these alternatives. This latter position demands struggle both individually and with others. As of yet, only a limited number of bisexuals have organized in this way. Is this so surprising?

Celibacy: sex and abstinence vs *struggle and choice*
Objectively, celibate lesbians question society's image of lesbians as excessively sexual women. Lesbians become celibate for a variety of reasons — loss or death of lover; fear of sexual involvement; illness; as a personal choice. However, in a sense, the determing factor is not as important as the position which it creates.

Celibate lesbians, like other celibates, show that, on a personal level, sex is not one of the essential factors in life. However, sex is (or shall we say sex becomes) one of the essential factors of life in order for us to perpetuate life and society.

Consciously or unconsciously, celibates help to point out existing tensions in society between theory and practice or between what society tells us and what actually happens. Celibates contradict the consistency or balance between a self-definition of oneself as sexual and a social definition of sexuality as 'active'. Celibates appear to accept neither. They ignore the separation which society attempts to maintain between the oversexed woman — a lesbian is a primary example — and the social function of women to reproduce sexually. Along with other lesbians, celibates do not occupy either position. Yet, from the traditional lesbian viewpoint, as well as the social lesbian viewpoint, if lesbians do choose celibacy, they appear to remove themselves from lesbians. Perhaps the following poem, 'Coming out Celibate' illustrates this position. It is not specifically about the celibate lesbian. However, it points out some of the feelings which are experienced by them.

Coming out Celibate

like men
so many women cannot imagine   friendship
                                creativity
                                existence
                                              without sexuality
or what passes for sexuality
so that when i say
                        i am celibate
smiles of embarrassment appear
and the subject is quickly changed
i am awarded
                        pity or contempt or simply bewilderment

that i should not do
                              sexual things with and to another person
preferably of the other gender
but anyway with someone for god's sake
since it's
abnormal-unnatural-undesirable-and especially immature
not to be dependent on someone
some of the time
for sexual satisfaction:
I'm celibate from lack of opportunity surely:
it couldn't be my very own consciously taken decision
                              could it?

because sleeping alone
even more than living alone
is seen as self denial
isn't it?

                              especially if i like it that way —
                              i just have to meet the right person
                              don't i?

we must all be seen in
                    couples
                    families, even "broken families"
                    collectives
                    some sort of relationship
all our lives
whether we like it or not
anything but as individuals being glad in our one-ness
celibacy is more about autonomy than specific
sexuality
celibacy is about choosing one's own
                              life style
                              friendships
                              ways of
                                        working
                                        doing
                                        being
and putting them all together
at different times
in different ways

imagine an epidemic of autonomous individuals
and you're on your way to
realizing a few feminist fantasies

© Astra

To reproduce or not to reproduce? that is the question –
lesbian mothers

More and more lesbians want to have children. Unfortunately, society places grave restrictions not only upon lesbian mothers who have children and want to keep them but also on lesbians who desire to 'mother' a child.

In society, women who raise children on their own or without men challenge the normal idea of the family. In addition to this, the lesbian mother has to cope with her rejection of being a 'real women' and, ultimately, a 'real mother'.

Some lesbians continue to live within well established families and are wives and mothers. Others find it difficult to live in this context and leave. If a lesbian mother leaves her family, she may or may not gain custody of her children. Her lesbianism may be used as evidence against her in a court case for custody of her children. Lesbianism may be a cause to believe that she is unsuitable as a mother. As a result, some lesbians do not gain custody of their children because they refuse to have a legal battle which could expose all.

Lesbians who desire to have children outside the family look for ways to become pregnant. Various methods are useful. One method is through artificial insemination by donor (AID). A doctor gives sperm from a sperm bank of donors to the future mother. She may either have the doctor inject her with the sperm or she may have her lover inject her with sperm. Although during the past year AID has become public knowledge through the media, this choice has been open to lesbians for many years. (During the course of this research, I met at least ten women who were mothers through AID.)

In order to be mothers, lesbians may also have sexual intercourse with men. Some lesbians call a man a 'stud' in this context. One lesbian who got pregnant in this way explained that she knew the man and felt that both of them could 'handle the experience'.

Problems do arise for lesbians who desire children and who are not able to get pregnant. They experience frustration in their attempt to fulfil a role or possibly a right, as some believe, which is theirs as a woman. Some lesbians felt that their thwarted attempts made them consider that they were being punished by society for being a lesbian and for remaining outside of the acceptable environments which are deemed necessary for mothers, family and husband, for example.

The occurrence of lesbian motherhood spans across all areas of the lesbian ghetto. Negative responses may come from other lesbians as well as society. Some feel that children are a 'burden', 'an added responsibility' or 'an unwanted challenge'. 'After all,' said one lesbian, 'one of the reasons why I became a lesbian was because I did not want to have children.' Gradually, however, the practice of lesbian motherhood is becoming important for many lesbians. At present, mothers meet with each other in certain areas of the ghetto to discuss the problems of this role. Several groups are organized by mothers for mothers. As a result they provide 'lesbian mums' with an increasing amount of social support from others. Lesbian mothers are becoming more and more able not only to cope with their role but also to transform it into a socially challenging one.

Conclusion – a movement towards ideology for social lesbians

This chapter has emphasized social lesbian practice, the gathering of a potentially political outlook. Lesbians are becoming aware of their critical position in relation to society. Yet, as we have seen, tradition still holds a firm grasp upon some social lesbians and affects their lesbian practice. However, it is during this particular group phase (social lesbianism) that lesbians become drawn to lesbian politics. Ideological tendencies appear. Political consciousness becomes clearer than before. There exists an awareness of the lesbian group struggle. All of these elements have a 'snowball effect' for lesbians. They help to create lesbianism as a social force in society or as a challenge to the total structure of society. 'Political momentum' gains speed.

In the next chapter, we will examine the implications of lesbianism as it develops into an ideological context from the struggle for lesbian consciousness. We will also look at the various divisive elements which create splits within the lesbian feminist position. Lesbian feminism emerges from social lesbianism and represents a shift towards ideology. While developing from a social form, it creates a new stage or phase in the development of lesbian consciousness. In effect, 'lesbian politics' become visible. Yet, we must remember that 'politics' can never exist in a 'pure form'. Therefore, we will see the lesbian struggle riddled with conflict or as involved in a contradictory process of growth, and it becomes a wonder that lesbian feminism has ever come into existence. Pregnant with tension, it mirrors all forms of struggle within and against society.

6 The emergence of political consciousness: lesbian feminism as an ideological form

Lesbianism is the negation of the concrete ideology of womenhood
... radical lesbians transform the personal struggle into a larger
social arena .... The revolutionary component of radical lesbian
thinking is the total institutional definition of women.[1]

Representing an historical progression from social lesbianism, lesbian
feminism[2] becomes increasingly more visible in Britain today. As a
small seed, lesbian feminism grows and develops with the emergence of
lesbianism into an 'ideological' stage or political phase. Through political
consciousness, lesbians stress not only group awareness but also group
struggle. Thus, lesbianism gains momentum as a social force, a threat to
be reckoned with. It begins to whittle down society's structure. In the
final analysis, it challenges the total structure of society and exposes all
types of oppression within the whole gamut of possible social
relationships.

The process of emergence and oppression

We have seen that prior to any political transition, lesbians went to gay
bars and clubs or joined lesbian and gay organizations. These particular
settings attempted and attempt to promote an understanding of lesbianism as an individual *cum* social problem. Also, they help lesbians to
evolve a group awareness among themselves. This also helps an individual lesbian's awareness of the group's potential. However, these
organizations or settings tend to have a stultifying effect upon radical
politics. They may condone the closet. The closet is inconsistent with a
high level of outness. (This factor is important for a political perspective.) In other words, the tendency towards radical politics for lesbians
implies not only group awareness and group 'outness' but also political

consciousness which is acquired as the group struggles against society.

Usually, because of the reformist character and specific social lesbian orientation of these organizations or settings, lesbians are not allowed by society to experience group struggle. They are sheltered from it, as their present situation calls for conformity to the ideals of homosexual reform and society's acceptance of lesbianism.

The notion of struggle

After reading the above paragraphs, you may rightly ask, 'What does struggle mean?' 'How does struggle (or can struggle) relate to lesbianism?' or 'What does struggle imply for lesbians and within a lesbian context?'

Generally, the notion of struggle indicates that there are two opposing forces which resist each other. For lesbians, as with many oppressed groups, struggle means that one develops with others a certain amount of resistance to society. It also implies that groups question how society organizes itself or how we structure social relationships.

As I indicated earlier, the structure of society is based on both material power and sexual power. On the one hand, material power emerges as money-acquiring. With this type of power, people become thing- rather than people-orientated. Material power is property-based. On the other hand, sexual power is established when the apparently dominant sex controls the apparently weaker sex. With this type of power, people become male-orientated. Sexual power is based upon what we believe to be human nature. Therefore aware groups challenge the use of power which is foisted upon them. Simply, oppression as it is experienced because of the use of power is made known. More often than not all forms of oppression, albeit connected, are not linked together. Struggle which results from the experience of oppression becomes splintered. Rather than a complicated web of human relationships, oppression and the resultant struggle against it appear together as a twisted structure with disconnected mazes. Yet, in reality, the struggle against oppression is a struggle against ourselves, our human relationships and our society which we help to create. Struggle is against not only the misuse of power, but power itself. Therefore, in order to see clearly, we must make links between the individual, groups and society. An understanding of the connections between all forms of social relationships may enable us to recognize power as well as how 'immune' we have become to its total use and influence in society.

Perhaps we are now becoming aware of the reasons why oppressed groups fail to make vital links between and among each other. Why, then, do the notions of oppression and of struggle appear to be removed from ourselves as well as from society?

The lesbian struggle – the restoration of personhood?

It seems that today more than ever before lesbians are coming out of the closet and talking publicly about their oppression. They confront those areas of society which put them down as being 'almost human' and 'less than "real" people'. Aware that society robs them of their human dignity, lesbians fight back to restore their personhood. This is the lesbian struggle, but, it is never removed from the context of total human struggle. As a result, and primarily because lesbians are women and perceive themselves as such, they establish connections with the struggle of all women. In this transition from group awareness to group consciousness, some ideologically orientated lesbians move towards radical politics.

Whatever form their politics takes depends upon the type of oppression which lesbian feminists appear to emphasize most. However, whether they are aware of it or not, as women as well as lesbian feminists, they have placed themselves firmly within the struggle for women's liberation. The key factor is that if lesbian feminism is to emerge, it must be closely related to women's progression in society. Simply, lesbian feminism becomes an integral part of the feminist movement.

But, what is the feminist movement? What are politically conscious women struggling against in society? How does this consciousness arise? What types of issues do they attempt to deal with? In order to make the vital links between the rise of lesbian consciousness and the rise of feminist consciousness, let us pause, think hard and put our feet on the ground.

Imagine a total picture of the complex process of the emergence of lesbianism and feminism, rather than static, isolated images. Let us place this picture within history. After all, the picture is sketched by the process of history. The consciousness of lesbians as well as the consciousness of women can be viewed as growing simultaneously. However, the total image of lesbianism is distorted. Representations of lesbians, although included within the total view, are not in full view, as are those of women. This is primarily because society has not allowed lesbians to be women. As a result, lesbians have created an almost unique women's consciousness for themselves as lesbians. Yet, I would contend that the rise of feminism and a political consciousness for all women has enabled lesbians to be included within a total view of women. Within our picture the distinct line between the image of les-bians and that of women has now become blurred. Images which were previously dissimilar are blended together. In reality, the lesbian/woman is no longer a hidden category as well as an opposing image to woman. The picture has changed, transformed itself even before us now. Prior to that change, lesbians were disguised as caricatures of men. Now the artist history, more exacting in her/his style, struggles to represent and to preserve only fine lines of distinction and similar shades of the same colour. Thus, lesbians are becoming illustrated more and more as women and less and less as isolated objects. Lesbians are becoming women. They have a place within our total picture. Amen to this analogy.

Lesbians have begun to break down the barriers which were created through years of separation from women and which, in turn, made them develop isolated images of themselves. In order to understand this argument, let us look briefly at the feminist movement today.

The women's liberation movement – theory and practice

Today, a women's liberation movement (WLM) exists. It has its roots in history from the first feminists. Feminism becomes a reality in society when women start questioning what it means to be a woman in society. As a group, feminists become critical of their inferior position. Whether black, white or coloured; whether heterosexual, homosexual or bisexual in orientations; whether married, single, divorced or widowed; whether manual worker, non-manual worker or unemployed; whether ruling-class, working-class or middle-class; or whether mothers, non-mothers or pregnant – women gradually experience the need to voice their particular oppression in company with other women. This experience effects a political base organization of sympathetic women, an aware-ness of the group's needs, a certain level of political consciousness and, ultimately, 'politics' for women.

In her discussion of the WLM in the USA, Freeman contends that there exists a consensus on 'two theoretical concerns'. The first is 'the feminist critique of society' and the second is 'the idea of oppression'.[3]

As women began to focus on relevant social arenas and to mobilize or organize around women's issues, women's problems and women's areas they demanded total equality with men. These claims emerged from their position as women. Their demands helped them to develop a type of 'women's politics'. Through concrete social practice, questioning with others their position as women, they effected new relationships among and between themselves. In other words, women viewed themselves as an oppressed group both economically — as a cheap labour force for capitalism whether outside the home or within it — and sexually as a 'second sex' in relationship to men.

Women began to criticize their unique, contradictory position within the established social order. Feminists or those who expressed political consciousness as women developed strategies and tactics to unite all women in the struggle against power. Power, they state, filters through all levels of human relationships. They developed informal networks of association, consciousness-raising groups, local campaigns and a body of literature — all which reflected their struggle with (not necessarily for) power.

A feminist view: power, society and women

Feminists have a particular view of power and of society. To them and to all women, society is oppressive. In other words, society uses power against and not for women. Society may be seen to be hierarchically organized not only through capitalism, in terms of workers and non-workers, but also through a co-existing patriarchy, in terms of men and women. More to the point and in light of the above view, how shall we see society or what is society?

Society is an ordering of human relationships or a system of how people relate to one another. Feminists become aware that society is not just 'something out there'. People, we, create society. In a contradictory sense, people make it. However, because people do not always agree with one another, conflict exists in society. Therefore, things change; society changes. Society is not a static thing but a developing process which is based upon the past (history), the present (conflict or struggle) and the future (attempts to resolve conflict). Yet, within the feminist view, a constant element exists of singular importance. It is power.

All social relationships are based upon power. Students of society who analyse power and its effect upon the organization of social life say 'Every social act is an exercise of power, every social relationship is a power equation and every social group or system is an organization of power',[4] or, 'Power is not a "thing" possessed by social actors but rather a dynamic process that occurs in all areas of social life . . . . It does not exist until social actors begin relating to one another in some manner.'[5] In order to understand power adequately, feminists look at it historically or with a hindsight view. They see it emerging in two ways according to the structure of society. It develops in terms of class relations and sex relations in a patriarchal capitalist order.

On the one hand, there are sex relations in which men are dominant and women subservient. This leads to a patriarchal view of society. It appears as oppressive to women, anti-women or anti-feminist. Women are oppressed because they reproduce and because reproduction may make them less productive. More importantly, because of their 'species-producing power', women are viewed as naturally inferior in relationship to men.

On the other hand, we have a system of class relations which divides workers from non-workers, owners of the means of production from non-owners. This leads to a capitalist view of society which appears as anti-worker or anti-the labouring class. In this view, workers are oppressed because they have to be productive in order to survive. In other words, in order to survive they must sell their labour for a wage to those who own the worker's means of producing and who control the way society, including the worker, produces for itself.

Feminists believe that these two types of social relations are based upon power, overlap in society and therefore, create the sexual division of labour. Simply, labour is also divided by sex. Men are viewed by society as primarily productive, making things necessary for themselves, their families and 'present' society to survive. Women are viewed as primarily reproductive, making babies necessary for society to survive in the future.

Traditionally, feminists use the family as a basic example of the sexual division of labour. Within it and through it, the above social roles and functions between men and women become clear. The sexual division of labour is based upon the basic biological difference between men and women as well as the divisions which exist in the labour process. Together these differences create divisions in society between sex and society; the private and the public; the family and society; home and workplace; women's work and men's work, and domestic labour and 'productive' labour.

In light of the above, feminists emphasize that patriarchal capitalism seems to divide worker from non-worker as well as productive labour from reproductive labour. Ultimately, through the sexual division of labour men and women become divided.

Historically, within the feminist critique of society, two major splits have become visible. These splits create two opposing camps which conflict over the issue of power. One camp, the Marxist feminists, have a tendency to criticize class relations and women's position within capitalism. The other camp, radical feminists, tend to direct their criticisms toward sex relations and women's position within patriarchy. (It is interesting to note here that in Britain during the past two years, a group, calling themselves Revolutionary Feminists, have emerged. They direct themselves towards criticizing both sex and class relations.) In whatever area each group directs their critique of society, they expose different forms of women's oppression.

Lesbianism: feminism or gay politics? Struggle with a double oppression

Since the development of a women's movement and the rise of feminist consciousness, many feminists assert that 'lesbianism is a logical alternative to a male partner's dominance'.[6] For many, lesbianism emerges as a specific challenge to sex relations. With this in mind, feminists directed an attack against male power or sexism and argued against the existence of patriarchy. From the radical feminist camp the notion of 'political lesbianism' was developed. Political lesbianism implied that women became lesbians in order to make a political statement. Basically, they rejected the oppression which they believed to be inherent in sexual relationships with men.

However, some women who had been previously straight were prepared to take the risk of being labelled 'lesbian'. Others who had 'always been lesbian', always lesbian-orientated, claimed that political lesbians were not 'real lesbians' like themselves. Real lesbians claimed that they had existed prior to the development of the women's movement, or any movement for that matter. They felt short-changed. After all, they had been struggling as lesbians long before these political ones 'came on the scene and stole the show'. Real lesbians were lesbians prior to the time when lesbianism became a political choice or 'fashionable' within the women's movement. Political lesbianism, as an alternative, threatened their position as real lesbians. Furthermore, it detracted from the meaningfulness of those intriguing years which were spent struggling to emerge from the closet.

Yet some real lesbians recognized that a women's political movement provided for them not only a certain degree of status as lesbians but also a level of consciousness with other women. Those with this awareness gradually grew in number and helped to form women's politics. Still others who were discouraged left. Together as a forming group, lesbians managed to play down the distinctions between each other and to join with feminist women in the struggle for liberation. With other women, lesbians attempted to establish the vital links between lesbianism and feminism. Both types of consciousness grew together.

However, this process was not problem-free. During the initial stages of the WLM or the beginnings of radical politics for women, women's consciousness, on the whole, seemed to conflict with lesbian consciousness. In other words, either straight women (who objectively held more power) oppressed lesbians for being gay or lesbians put down heterosexual women for being straight and mirroring sexual power in society. Some, both gay and straight, resolved the tension, while others fled from conflict and the movement itself.

The rise of lesbian consciousness also led to the notions of gay politics, gay consciousness and the emergence of a gay movement. Within this political arena, lesbians, together with gay men, mounted an attack against a dominant heterosexual society. With a keen awareness as homosexuals or a sexual minority, they became critical of society's oppression of them. In effect, lesbians whose gay consciousness appeared to be more developed than their feminist consciousness helped to organize the Gay Liberation Front (GLF).[7]

As lesbian consciousness had conflicted with feminist consciousness, so also its fate was conflict with gay consciousness. GLF lesbians[8] felt oppressed as women within GLF and reflected a secondary status within the total gay struggle in relationship to gay men. It became clear that their position in GLF was a real reflection of their position as women in society. Within this movement, they were not only apeing an oppressive society but continuing their own oppression as women. Effectively, this struggle accelerated the development of GLF lesbians' awareness as women and exposed anti-feminist politics within the gay movement itself.

As a result many lesbians left GLF. Today gay politics still exist in Britain. Yet one has only to read through some of the literature (*Gay News, Gay Left*, etc.) to see the predominant male-orientation. Whether they are aware of it or not, lesbians who were previously more gay-orientated than feminist-orientated have learned a lesson from history. Unless they themselves are anti-feminist, they tend now to be more aware of their similarities with other women than with gay men. They may also come to realize that they will experience less of a struggle as lesbians and women within a women's movement and more of a struggle as lesbians and women within a male-orientated gay movement. However they choose to become political depends upon how aware they are of being doubly oppressed, as women and as lesbians.

The WLM and the Sixth Demand

Since the 1970 Oxford Conference, which accelerated the growth of women's consciousness in Britain, women's conferences have been regularly organized throughout the country. These conferences serve an integrative function for the WLM and help to create and establish networks of communication for women. Usually conferences are organized around women's issues or demands such as equal pay, equal education, etc. These demands provide the basis for a unifying force as women. Women's demands focus upon the problems that women experience in a society which furthers women's oppression.

With the rise of feminism in 1970 four demands of the WLM were set up. They dealt with the issues of equal pay, equal education and opportunity, twenty-four hour nurseries, and free contraception and abortion on demand. Four years later, at the National Conference of the WLM in Edinburgh, two more demands were added to the aims of the WLM — legal and financial independence for all women and an end to discrimination against lesbians — the right of women to a self-defined sexuality. The WLM became committed to these demands. The inclusion of the lesbian demand reflected that lesbians were an active part of the feminist movement. They had linked up their consciousness with women's.

Gradually feminists supported the rights of women to a self-defined sexuality — a sexuality hidden under layers of isolation through years of oppression. For lesbian feminists, the struggle for lesbian liberation is not viewed as their primary concern nor is it the one necessary form of consciousness for women. Rather, it is part of the total movement forward and it is most explicitly or necessarily linked up with all women's struggles – class, racial, sexual, and so on.

For all feminists, any social issue that reflects contradictions in a male-dominated capitalist system is a *real issue*. The term women-identified women became a direct attack against the established order.

Lesbian feminism: a wedge?

As we have seen previously, lesbianism objectively sets up a whole series of contradictions or creates tensions in society. If lesbians become conscious of what their position demonstrates or what it represents, if lesbianism emerges politically or if the majority of lesbians emerge from an ideological standpoint as primarily lesbian feminists, then lesbianism manifests itself as a social force. In other words, at a conscious level lesbianism not only contradicts society visibly but also questions the previously 'invisible' roots of its structure.

Recall my prior discussion of the tensions which lesbianism exposes. Now apply these objective contradictions to lesbian feminism. You will see that lesbian feminism polarizes the divisions between class relations as well as sex relations. It exposes not only power relations between social classes but also power relations between men and women. More simply, it points out that for an oppressive society its theory (what society tells us) and its practice (what its people actually do) do not at all relate. Oppression causes this divide, while power makes oppression possible.

In particular lesbian feminism reflects the contradictory position of society[9] and therefore of all women and people within it. In close relationship to the position of women, lesbianism uncovers divisions which exist between women as reproducers and women as producers.

Lesbianism and more explicitly lesbian feminism contradicts society because of the following:

> With society's idea of *women as primarily reproducers* (making babies)
>> Lesbians appear as
>>> almost *non-reproducers* in relationship to women
>>> and therefore, *secondary reproducers vis à vis*

the primary ones (women),
and
as *reproducers in relationship to men* (who
are non-reproducers, full stop).

With society's idea of *women as secondarily producers* (making things)

Lesbians appear as
more productive in relationship to women –
many have to support themselves and do not
rely on a male (husband's) wage,
and
less productive in relationship to men –
ultimately, lesbians as women are part
of the female labour force which is
secondary to the male labour force.

Thus, lesbian feminism drives a wedge between society's theory – the structure of people's, especially women's lives – and its practice – what women actually do.

It should be easy to see that the development of lesbian feminism has emerged through struggle. Earlier in this chapter, we saw that the rise of lesbian feminism conflicted with the emergence of feminist consciousness as well as gay consciousness. Although diminishing, the effects of these conflicts still exist today.

In this context we will add another type of consciousness which, I would contend, is as important as all forms of human consciousness. It is class consciousness. Although class consciousness has been a dominant notion, as well as dominating form of consciousness in the political arena, it, not surprisingly, has also had an affect upon lesbian consciousness.

Lesbian separatists vs lesbian allies: a contradiction within lesbian feminism?

In recent years, two major political forces split lesbian feminism. These forces also mirror in a smaller way the two opposing camps within the WLM. Both forces or lesbian political groups oppose as well as divide lesbian feminism. The two groups are lesbian separatists and lesbian allies. Before we discuss the distinctions between the two, we should look at how these divisions come about within the total lesbian feminist framework.

Lesbian feminism (LF) is a struggle against power in a patriarchal capitalist order. It develops a two-pronged attack against society. But because feminists have generally developed an attack which is based on their own isolation and vulnerability as women, they are not, or should not be, seeking *power for themselves*. The irony is that feminists become powerful and emerge as a political force only by recognizing their powerlessness or their position of being powerless, whether in terms of class relations or sex relations. The contradiction is that as a social force, feminists represent 'group powerlessness'. Therefore one of the aims of the WLM is to be aware of the group's position and to struggle against power by refusing it for themselves. LF having emerged from this historical standpoint struggle to do likewise — to renounce power — in all its insidious forms. Yet, while lesbian feminism implies resisting and furthermore renouncing power, lesbian separatists and lesbian allies, who are supposedly politically conscious lesbians, take power for themselves.

Lesbian separatists, although initially in a minority, get power by establishing the principle that lesbian feminism is the most important type of consciousness for women as well as for lesbians. Reminiscent of lesbian chauvinism or this type of lesbian practice at a pre-political stage of awareness, separatists created the slogan 'Lesbian is Best' in the WLM. Lesbian separatism brings with it a hierarchical power structuring of women in their struggle for liberation. Ultimately, separatism aims to effect this principle in a society which will be based upon women or a matriarchal order.

Separatists' main attack is against male power, sexism and anti-feminism — all of which are the results of a patriarchal society. While denying the importance of criticizing class relations, separatists oppose sex relations. Patriarchy rather than capitalism is their main target. Yet, within the context of the *total* struggle against power relations (patriarchy and capitalism), they are a divisive force. They are feminists, lesbian feminists, yet they deny a basic feminist principle — class relations oppress women. In the last analysis, separatism is anti-feminist.

Another anti-feminist tendency or position is illustrated through lesbian allies. They are lesbian feminists who ally themselves closely to the left and join the dominating struggle against capitalism. Here we see that their class consciousness comes into conflict with their feminist and/or lesbian consciousness. While struggling against class relations, lesbian allies reject the importance of actively challenging sex relations. Like separatism, they are a divisive force for lesbian feminism.

By allying themselves with a male-orientated and men-dominated class struggle, they reflect their oppressed position as women within society. However, as we have seen, women do experience a particular form of oppression in capitalism through the sexual division of labour. Having a class consciousness, lesbian allies are acutely aware of this division. It should be no surprise that they carry this division into the struggle and reflect this sexual division in the class struggle. Yet, they deny that patriarchy, sex relations and male power not only exist but oppress women. A principle of feminism may be represented by the equation, Patriarchy = Society's Structure (sex relations). Therefore, feminism necessitates an active critique or struggle on that level. Feminism also necessitates the acceptance of the equation, Capitalism = Society's Structure (class relations). Lesbian allies will only accept the latter feminist equation. For them, Patriarchy = Culture.[10] They reject a necessary feminist principle and transform it on their terms (class bias). In this way, they too are anti-feminist.

Separatists and allies taken together reflect the tensions within the lesbian struggle as well as within the total resistance against power. If really and not apparently united as lesbian feminists, these two groups have the potential to expose contradictions which are rooted in society and which further divide people from people. Therefore, as the backdrop of the various forms of anti-feminism recedes, through struggle, conflict and protest, progressive change will be effected.

The lesbian feminist ghetto: a case study

The final section of this chapter will be a brief discussion of a particular lesbian feminist ghetto. The discussion illustrates ideological lesbianism in seed form. As a detailed account, it shows quite clearly how lesbian feminist consciousness emerged from the women's liberation movement (WLM) and also how lesbianism is consciously lived out. All the following data was collected for research[11] which was completed during 1973-7 in London.

It was in a south London borough that this particular lesbian feminist ghetto emerged. Since this account was written it has dissolved due to the demolition of most of the houses in the area concerned.

The lesbian feminist ghetto lasted approximately six years. It involved directly approximately 50 lesbian feminists as residents and indirectly approximately 150 feminists as non-residents and including some straight feminists. Within the radius of half a mile the ghetto emerged, grew and developed as a centre for lesbian feminist activity not only within their particular neighbourhood but also within London.

Housing arrangements and employment practices developed as did the somewhat localised yet evolving feminist consciousness. Within this neighbourhood, most of the lesbian feminists lived in houses that were located in four terraces on two city streets. The streets were parallel to each other, had approximately the same number of houses (40) and were about one street block distance from each other.

The houses all had facilities for cold or hot and cold running water, electricity, gas and an outside lavatory. None of them was centrally heated. Besides the lesbian feminists, the terraces were also occupied by 'traditional' working-class families – or what sociologists believe to be traditional working-class families – with approximately two children per family unit. There were 18-20 family units. Ages of the parents ranged from mid-20s to 40s. The children's ages ranged from 0+-16. Although all the houses were owned by the local council, the terms of occupation varied. Occupants consisted of either squatters or council tenants. There were no owner-occupiers on these specific blocks. The majority of lesbian feminists were squatters, while the majority of other residents in the area were council tenants. Only 3 family units appeared to be squatting.

Most of the lesbian feminists in the area were either employed as manual workers or they were claimants. Some were students. Skilled or professional workers were in a minority of only 3 in number. One of the few professionally trained lesbian feminists remained a claimant during her residency (5 years) in the ghetto.

The roots of the actual spatial designation for the ghetto can be found during 1971. At that time, a lesbian feminist, 22 years old and a claimant, who was active in the WLM became a squatter in one of the houses. Through friends, she was informed that the local council had been vacating these houses for a new re-development scheme which was to begin in three years' time (1974). When this information was given to her, she was also aware, through rumours in the neighbourhood, that the local council had also been effecting cutbacks in its expenditure and that re-development would be postponed an additional 2 years (1976). Demolition of the structures would probably take place in the distant future. On the basis of this information and along with the fact that houses in the area were being vacated, the squatting began. Ten houses on one street remained vacant during this initial stage, while on the other street, eight houses were and would be vacant.

The spatial potential for the establishment of the ghetto became a reality. Although the conscious development of the ghetto remained hidden or invisible until at least half the lesbian-feminists (25) resided in the area within 6 months time, lesbian feminist practice emerged. As a result, lesbian feminist consciousness became active. After the intial lesbian feminists became residents, the news of the ghetto spread within the WLM's communication network. It is interesting to note that the above lesbian feminists received information about the ghetto through this same communication network.

Squats, as lesbian households, were set up by lesbians who were homeless for a variety of reasons (i.e. they were unable to pay for rented accommodation due to unemployment, disability or other reasons; split from lover and desire to get away from it all; desire to live with other lesbian feminists in an area of heightened political activity or desire to squat). In these houses lesbian feminists established relationships with one another as friends or lovers. Often former lovers were included within the area. Children of lesbian feminists also lived in houses with their mothers.

As lesbian feminists, a social base, were organizing in this area of London, a social force emerged. Lesbian feminist practice developed a unique system of integrating networks and relationships both within the lesbian feminist ghetto, with other lesbian feminists and local residents and outside the ghetto with the WLM. A Women's Centre, initially located in one of the specified houses, was set up in 1972 as an information service to provide *any woman*, but usually women in the area, with knowledge about many issues of the WLM. The dynamics of this centre also established a textured system not only between women in the general area, feminist and pre-feminist,[12] and the WLM in London but also between lesbian feminists in the ghetto and feminists in local areas. Regularly, women who were not fully committed to the WLM and who experienced a crisis period, such as divorce, rape, battering from husband, would seek support and information from the Women's Centre or from other lesbian feminists in the ghetto. It was also possible for women new to the area to seek out information about housing accommodation and possibly to be housed in the immediate area, provided that there were vacancies.

A few core lesbian feminists remained in the ghetto for the span of its existence (6 years) and worked closely together in the lesbian feminist ghetto and the WLM network. Others, who appeared to be more transient, left the ghetto for a variety of reasons (job, split with lover, quarrel with friend, to live with friend/s or lover/s outside the ghetto, change in lesbian feminist practice, etc.)

A reactive tendency towards separatism, although a potential in the early stages of the ghetto's development, emerged in the ghetto within one year of its initial establishment. Consistently, there were two distinguishable tendencies in the ghetto. They were the radical lesbian tendency and the lesbian separatist tendency.[13] It was with the development of the latter, reactive tendency (separatism) that divisions became visible.

On the one hand, separatism progressed as a unifying, albeit reactive force for sympathetic social agents (separatists). On the other hand, it served as an oppressive force for those who upheld feminist practice. Within the framework of the WLM as well as the lesbian feminist struggle, some feminist theorists could contend that the separatist tendency in this context effected the ultimate destruction of this lesbian feminist ghetto, brought out the contradictions in some areas of lesbian feminist practice and caused increasing conflict both within the ghetto and without as this tendency grew and received support from sympathetic lesbians.

In relationship to other residents, greater integration was possible between the lesbian feminists and other local women than with the men residents, with the exception of the separatists who did not have any contact with men. Lesbian feminists would engage in a certain amount of child-minding for local mothers. As I mentioned previously, local women during period of crisis became aware that there were other women — the lesbian feminists — who would be willing to give support. Of course, this fact varied according to the women residents' contact with the lesbian feminists as well as their own ideas about lesbianism in general. Most of the residents in the area knew each other, lesbians and other occupants alike. The reaction to the lesbians varied from acceptance to open hostility and, sometimes, harassment. Hostility was evidenced by slogans which were spray-painted on local bill-boards, such as 'Dykes Out' or 'Lessies Go Home'. Generally, the relationship between the residents and the lesbian feminists appeared to be one of indifference. The incidents of open hostility were not common. Yet, intimidation did exist and one incident is worth mentioning in this context.

The pub war: Teddies[14] vs *Dykes*

In June 1977, immediately prior to the demise of the lesbian feminist ghetto, there was an incident which could be viewed as a 'pub war' between the lesbian feminists and a local gang of Teds. Hostility escalated when the local Teds experienced invasion of their territory by the lesbian feminists. Gradually what initially emerged as harassment by the Teds developed into street violence. This particular gang tended to mobilize their activities from specific areas in the locality. These areas, however, changed from time to time. It was when they chose to gather at a local pub near to the ghetto as well as in the centre of lesbian feminists' leisure activities, that trouble began. Confrontation became inevitable. Within three weeks of the Teds' attempt to take over the pub, violence occurred. Lesbian feminists' leisure activities were held on Wednesday, Friday, Saturday and Sunday in an upstairs room in the pub. Attendance at these leisure events ultimately precipitated a 'pub war'. The Teds physically attacked the lesbian feminists. Often lesbian feminists were harassed or followed home by the Teds. Some were beaten up. In the end, due to the concern of some of the local residents, police control was initiated. One lesbian feminist recalls:

> 'It was incredible to think that after all of us were finished boozing that we'd go out there and we might get bashed up. One night the police came out. I guess they heard that there might be trouble and escorted us all home. It really wasn't like that but the pandas were all out in full force and I remember seeing two policewomen. Imagine that! Police protection for dykes!'

Due to the management's lack of support for the continuation of their leisure activities and the fact that two lesbian feminists were seriously injured in the pub war, the lesbians abandoned the idea of remaining associated with this particular local pub. The Teds won out. In their battle for territorial space which they viewed as theirs, they managed to banish the lesbian feminists. Later, however, another pub in the area became the centre of activities. But, as I stated earlier, the lesbian feminist ghetto now no longer exists.

Possibly in this chapter the reader has become aware of the vast implications of lesbian feminism as well as the position of lesbianism in the feminist struggle against power. The following chapter will provide a general overview of the basic themes. It will also bring together crucial elements which are necessary for us in our understanding of lesbianism and, possibly, of women's position within it. It will offer a new look on society. Finally, in the my final remarks, I will tie together some loose ends and, I hope, provide a framework for future studies in this area.

Afterword – The lesbian struggle: sex *vs* class or nature *vs* labour?

A major aim of this book has been to challenge not only ideas about lesbianism but also ideas about women, sexuality and 'human nature'. The following section presents some seed ideas which are consistent with those developed from my research. However, many of these ideas were conceived after the major part of my study was carried out.

My theoretical position emerged as a direct consequence of the general subject area: lesbianism. It reflects the view that lesbianism as a particular historical position has the potential to create for women forms of consciousness which were hitherto unheard-of and which were often mislabelled as false.

In studying the theoretical alternative, one should be mindful of an important underlying principle. For women, lesbianism is one of the only social roles which are not capable of being performed by a man (although in the case of a man who becomes a transsexual and who then chooses a lesbian stance, the singularity of this position is challenged). Thus, lesbianism emerges not only as a totally contradictory position in terms of human production, but furthermore (and possibly in time, more importantly) as an historical reality and threat which exposes women's unique relationship to power.

The way of looking at these ideas in a consistent manner has been through an analysis of power. Conflicts, struggles or contradictory forces which emerge in society were examined. Society is defined as a system of social relationships which are based upon power. In light of the major aim stated above, the final aim of this book is to challenge ideas about power. Power is possible only for and through material beings. Although it may seem surprising to many, lesbianism relates to power. It is a direct challenge to women's position which is determined by power relationships. My ultimate argument will be that the social emergence of lesbianism is rooted in the organization of power rather than in individual lesbians. Thus far, the roots of this position have

157

been put forward.

As an historical phenomenon, lesbianism changes through conflict and struggle. As a social force, lesbianism contradicts 'nature', or what we conceive to be 'human nature', as well as society. Lesbianism opposes the fundamental forms of power which are based on 'human nature' and human labour. As a result, lesbianism upsets an ideological balance which has developed from the notions of sex and class in sociology. It reflects the conflict between male power and material power.

Also lesbianism reflects the view that history is a social process, because it emerges from a traditional stage to a social stage and finally to an ideological stage. This book has emphasized the second stage. The main justification for this emphasis is that social lesbianism may characterize the lesbian experience for the majority of contemporary lesbians. In other words, although this study points out that some social lesbians may be orientated towards either a traditional view of themselves or an ideological one, they are most definitely socially orientated. Perhaps social lesbianism is the most dominant form which appears in today's society. Yet a transition is occurring. As tradition is being progressively overruled, the seeds of ideology are being sown.

Looking at the first stage of lesbianism, we see elements of traditional ideas. The emphasis is upon the individual lesbian who tends to see herself as a 'sick lesbian'. Thus, she not only reflects but accepts society's view that lesbianism is a disease or a social disorder. Traditional lesbians are very likely to live a closeted existence as well as to become socially isolated from other lesbians. As a result, they are politically impotent and unable to challenge society. Their acceptance of tradition makes them unaware of any potential which lesbians have as a group. The social lesbian stage appears when lesbians establish a sense of group awareness. Gradually, lesbians emphasize a group context rather than an individual one. The emphasis provides them with a framework which is potentially political. By appearing as less closeted and more open than traditional lesbians, social lesbians begin to challenge social norms and to create a social problem in society.

Yet two somewhat opposing views occur within social lesbianism. These views present us with a conflicting process. While orientated towards tradition, 'sick but not sorry' lesbians emerge from the past and move towards social acceptability. While generally group orientated, the 'sorry but not sick' type have a tendency towards 'politics' or group resistance. Together, both types represent social lesbianism. As their group awareness as well as group identity grows, they gather the power to confront society. Their present stage of challenge breeds resistance and a shift towards ideology, the final stage.

Today, this final stage of lesbianism appears in seed form. Lesbianism at a politically conscious level gradually becomes linked up to the total struggle against women's subservient position in society. While their emphasis is upon group struggle, lesbian feminists expose major divisions in the struggle against power. Like social lesbians, lesbian feminists are divided as a group. Unlike the divisions within social lesbianism, the divisions within ideological lesbianism reflect a certain level of false consciousness or a degree of political infighting among those who are supposedly conscious. As a result, two types of groups emerge. While lesbian allies maintain the importance of class relations, lesbian separatists place priority upon sex relations. Yet, both groups together illustrate a lesbian feminist stance. This stance is a progression towards political consciousness for lesbians. This type of consciousness represents a consciousness with all women as well as with other oppressed groups in society. The following diagram illustrates the development of lesbianism in society. From Figure 1 we see that the emergence of lesbianism in society and the rise of lesbian consciousness point out some interesting ideas about society.

A major contention of this book is that lesbianism opposes all forms of power relations as they exist now in society. The basic assumption about power is that it not only filters through all social relationships but also emerges historically in two ways – through patriarchy and through capitalism; with the sexual organization of power and the material organization of power or through sex relations and through class relations. We have also assumed that these two systems of social relations produce a sexual division of labour. We have seen how lesbianism contradicts the sexual division of labour. The sexual division of labour is created by the labour process within society itself. But more importantly the division of labour, from which this sexual division originates, occurs within what some would term the dialectics of nature.[1]

In the following section, I will explain what the term 'dialectics' means as well as expose another dialectic which has been consistently overlooked and which could expand our understanding of power in society. As a result, the next few sections may prove to be quite complex and possibly tedious for some readers. However, the text will be presented as clearly as possible, and the accompanying diagrams should serve to clarify the proposed theoretical position.

Figure 1 *The stages of lesbianism*

	Traditional	Social	Ideological
emphasis upon	individual lesbian	group context (sub-culture)	group politics
who is she?	'sick lesbian' (accepts society's view of her as sick)	social lesbian, either 'sick but not sorry' or 'sorry but not sick'	lesbian feminist
level of emergence	from isolation (appears in closet)	from group awareness (begins to come out)	from struggle (totally out)
type of con-sciousness	apolitical (politically impotent)	pre-political (potentially political)	political (a social force)
society's response	lesbianism is a disease – isolate it or cure it	lesbianism is treated as a social problem	lesbianism is a threat to society
conflicts within particular stage	conflicts are mini-mized because lesbian accepts society	conflict between	conflict between conflict between

'Sick but
not sorry'
tradition
sick
closet
sexual
   preference
social
social
   acceptance
group
   awareness

'Sorry but
not sick'
social
group awareness
out
public notion
  of sex
challenge sick
  view
ideological
some feminist
  links made

Allies
anti-feminist
emphasize
  class rela-
  tions
'class
  power'

Separatists
anti-class
emphasize
  sex rela-
  tions
'male
  power'

The dialectics of power: sex vs class or nature vs labour?

Throughout this discussion the implication that patriarchy and capitalism co-exist has been made. Historically, patriarchy and capitalism appear at society's roots or are mutually supportive forms of how society organizes power. However, I would contend that they not only co-exist but also contradict one another. Together, they are created by and present us with the *dialectics of power*. This does not create a dualistic approach. Rather, a dialectical approach emerges for an understanding of women's oppression.

In other words, if we consider the position of women in relation to the opposition between patriarchy and capitalism (or patriarchy/capitalism) rather than in terms of patriarchal capitalism, we see some interesting implications. This 'structural opposition' sets up a further, more far-reaching, division than one which was previously upheld under patriarchal capitalism – the sexual division of labour. In other words, patriarchy/capitalism is a unique power system as well as a self-opposing system of social relations. Taken separately, each element of power is closely intertwined, yet each opposes the other. Together, both elements produce a sexual division of power as well as reflect the dialectics of power. The dialectic of power exposes conflicts between the power to reproduce – human reproductive power – and the power to produce – human productive power; reproduction and production; the ability to make babies and the ability to make things; 'natural power' and labour power and, ultimately, nature and society.

As of yet, feminist theory has not proposed patriarchy/capitalism as being a system of mutually supportive yet contradicting systems or forms of power relations. Thus far, the feminist struggle for ideas about power, conflict, women's oppression, etc. illustrates either a somewhat male-orientated Marxist approach or a somewhat female-orientated separatist approach. We have seen this demonstrated in the lesbian feminist struggle. The battle for the correct feminist theory goes on. Yet, this struggle exposes conflicts between too much emphasis on either the dialectics of sex through radical feminism[2] or the dialectics of nature through Marxist feminism.

Feminist theory creates insight into the conflict between patriarchy and capitalism; male power and material power; sex relations and class relations, or the concepts of 'sex' and 'class'. The problem is that either of the two theoretical camps tends to treat the other group's position merely as a 'cultural critique'. Simply, on the one hand, feminists say patriarchy is a structural issue, while capitalism is a cultural issue. On the other hand, Marxists say capitalism is *the* structural issue, while patriarchy represents a cultural phenomenon. Neither group locates patriarchy and capitalism *together* as the structure of society. Therefore, conclusions are made that the class struggle takes priority over the women's struggle or vice versa. A nice safe compromise[3] can, however, be made between Marxists and feminists. This compromise, the sexual division of labour, has developed primarily from the former's debate around the political economy of women. However, in the last analysis, the class struggle, the division of labour under capitalism, etc. take priority over and above the women's struggle as well as all other struggles such as race.

Therefore, a new analysis is necessary in order to clear up the stale air which is presently causing theoretical as well as political sickness. Rather than emphasize the concept of power in relationship to sex and class, why not look at power in relationship to the more fundamental issues which both feminists and Marxists see as its origin: *nature* and *labour*. More simply, let us examine 'natural power' and 'labour power'. However, this examination does not end up full stop as does an examination of the sexual division of labour which emerges from the dialectics of nature. Our current examination is not solely concerned with the dialectics of nature. Rather, we are concerned with the dialectics of power as it creates and is created by both the dialectics of sex and the dialectics of nature. This analysis is capable of linking up all forms of human oppression, human struggle and human division. It not only opens wide a discussion of sex, class, nature, labour and power but also exposes how each area of human life opposes each other as well as itself.

What do we mean by dialectics?

Dialectics is a way of looking at society and ourselves. It may also be a way of thinking about how everything grows and changes with growth. Developing from early Greek thinkers, dialectics is now a science, an 'objective' (as well as subjective) way of looking at social change. The key to dialectics is the process of change. Change occurs through conflict and ultimately through opposition. Therefore human growth occurs only in and through conflict. Conflict implies struggle between opposing forces. And we know, if we look at ourselves, we grow, develop and change our positions, our ideas, our perspective, etc. usually through struggle, challenge or opposition. The end product is the unity between opposition or 'opposing forces'. Some call this unity synthesis, others call it compromise. In other words, we have two forces which conflict (a positive one and a negative one):

POSITIVE FORCE *vs* NEGATIVE FORCE

but

POSITIVE FORCE + NEGATIVE FORCE = Unity (SYNTHESIS)
of FORCES

These equations illustrates very basically what the term 'dialectics' means. Within this view, change occurs only in and through *opposition*.

Marx upheld that the dialectics revealed 'universal laws' of human life. In fact, the dialectical process, laws of change and development, was the only real, essential part of 'man'.[4] Humans have the power to go beyond themselves. They not only 'objectify themselves' in thought by thinking but also 'objectify themselves' in the world by doing. However, these humans' theory and practice and, more specifically, society's theory and practice, as we have seen, tend not to relate. If they do, they continually conflict. Yet, conflict causes social development and ultimately, human growth.

Now if we translate the above ideas to the notion of history, we may set up the following equation:

HUMAN HISTORY + POWER = STRUGGLE, CONFLICT,
OPPOSITION

On a 'lower' level, the equation would read like this:

HUMAN INDIVIDUAL NEEDS + THE POWER TO FULFILL
THESE NEEDS (PRODUCE) = STRUGGLE, CONFLICT, ETC.

The first equation show us that throughout all human history – our history – society has consistently been inconsistent. In other words, society has always changed, developed, grown, etc. through conflict. This knowledge tells us what happens when unity occurs by the coming together of differences or opposing forces in society. On the one hand we have tradition. On the other hand we have conflict with tradition. The result is social change.

In a similar sense but on an individual level, we are all walking contradictions. And probably, more often than not, what we feel is not

usually consistent with what we do. Our needs come into conflict with
the fulfillment of our needs. And yet, we grow in this way. Simply,
theory contradicts practice. The notion of dialectics reveals to us, thus
far, all that we are as humans:

HUMAN BEINGS + POWER = STRUGGLE

or

NEEDS + SATISFACTION OF NEEDS = CONFLICT

However, the above discussion is centred around what some would
term the dialectics of nature.[5] Within this view, the dialectics of nature
is not only the *major* dialectics of human life but also *the* overriding
principle of human life. In other words, opposition is human life.
Marxists believe that this opposition has been twisted all out of proportion and that as a result, history creates a class struggle which divides
people from people. Opposition (dialectics), although a part of human
'nature' – the only 'part' of human 'nature'[6] – is out of control.
Instead of using this method of opposition, dialectical reasoning, for
ourselves, we have throughout history used it against ourselves. Thus,
we have a society based upon human power rather than human needs.
Marxists believe that if we eliminate the contradiction between human
needs and human power we will eliminate social conflict and we will
have a classless society.

Although the proponents of the above views do not uphold the
concept 'human nature', they appear to accept its existence merely by
opposing it. In other words, the dialectics of nature while opposing
'human nature' posits 'it'. Simply, in their attempt to contradict
nature, Marxists initially must establish some form of 'it' in order to
oppose 'it'. This is because they believe that conflict is inherent in
human life. I would contend that conflict, opposition, etc. is not
inherent in human life and that we have made it so. Opposition is not
human nature. Therefore, rather than

HUMAN BEINGS + POWER = STRUGGLE

I would contend that the crucial equation is

HUMAN BEINGS + STRUGGLE = POWER

The implication of the above is that neither power nor contradiction
(opposition) are inherent in human beings, society or human history.
We believe that power is a social phenomenon which appears

'transhistorically'. In other words, it has always been a social fact. Yet, it is or it may also appear to be a fixed, historical form in the emergence or development of human people who conflict with one another and who develop hierarchies in relationship to each other. On the one hand we see that power exists, while on the other hand, we never question why it exists or furthermore, if it is necessary that it exists. In this view, power and not just 'human nature' needs to be questioned.

In our lives, contradictions exist between what we believe to be 'human nature' and what 'is' human nature as well as what we believe to be society and what society really is. We have seen this especially in relationship to lesbianism in society. Yet in reality both our 'nature' and our 'society' are the same – creation of 'power'. In other words, in our minds power has become that which is the ability to oppose, to contradict and, ultimately, to transform what is human – ourselves.

The notion of power exposes the contradictions between conflicts of sex and conflicts of nature; between 'natural' power and social or 'labour' power or between 'nature' and society. For we, as humans, have the ability not only to survive, as do other forms of life, but also to create our own means to survive. Our survival becomes closely linked up with the organization of our human labour, as we create ways of 'going beyond ourselves'. Simply, we place the power of our human 'nature' in line with the power of our human labour. We want to be productive; we are productive. Yet, in all of this creative process, power is the constant – not our nature, our sex, our labour. But, we consistently use power against ourselves. Social power not only implies but *is* the misuse of power. Social power is the root of all social inconsistency. It ruptures theory from practice and practice from theory. It alienates 'nature' from society and society from 'nature'. Ultimately, it divides people from people in their struggle for 'it' (power).

In light of the above, I would contend that POWER IS THE MAJOR CREATOR OF SOCIAL CONFLICT. Power, not nature, is the primary dialectic. Within this view, the dialectics of power replaces the dialectics of nature. In other words, the most fundamental opposition in society is reflected in how society organizes power. The most fundamental way society organizes power is through 'nature' *and* 'labour' or the dialectics of sex *and* the dialectics of nature. While both oppose each other (thus far in the course of human history), together they have the potential to transform the structure of society or to eliminate power. Why don't we take 'a leap of faith' and imagine what it would be like if power was eliminated?

Realistically, it will take another book to describe in detail the above 'seed' theory about power. However, the basic framework will be provided below.

Power and division

Basically, power in society sets up divisions within and between the forces of 'nature', sex, 'labour' and 'the social'. All these notions are seen to develop as historical necessities.

Let us look at divisions that are established and maintained within each concept or notion as well as between each notion.

NATURE	There is a basic difference between (1) needs and power, (2) reproduction and production or (3) survival and the means or ability to survive. (Sex opposes nature.)
AS A RESULT SEX	Men and women are 'naturally' different from one another. Women reproduce and men produce. (Labour opposes sex, ultimately, nature).
AS A RESULT LABOUR	There is a fundamental difference between the needs of 'nature' and the needs of 'society'; the desire to produce and being productive; producing self and producing society; reproductive labour and productive labour. (Power opposes labour.)
AS A RESULT SOCIAL	Power is fundamental in society. Nature, sex, labour, the social oppose one another. Nature is static, unchanging. Sex is divorced from society ('privatized'). Labour divisions are seen to be necessary. Society is divided by power.

Oppression runs rampant in society. Power sets up hierarchical and therefore conflicting relationships. Power oppresses all those who are in minimal possession of it (in light of the above social realities).

The dialectics of sex is ultimately based upon 'nature' or the means of reproduction. Divisions are set up between 'reproducers' and non-reproducers, women and men. The dialectics of nature is ultimately based upon 'labour' or the means of production. Divisions are set up between 'producers' and non-producers, working class and ruling class. Both dialectics are created by conflicts in the human struggle for power.

We may represent the above in the following way:

	NATURE	*vs*	LABOUR	MEANS TO
SURVIVAL	*vs*		*vs*	SURVIVE
	SEX	*vs*	SOCIETY	

Or, we may wish to represent the divisions within each 'dialectic':

NATURE	*vs*	LABOUR
Needs		Power
Desire to produce		Production
vs		*vs*
SEX		SOCIAL
Needs		Power
Desire to reproduce	*vs*	Reproduction

(DIALECTICS OF POWER)

On the one hand, each division (nature, sex, labour, social) which is created by the dialectics of power reflects not only 'its' particular needs and abilities (power) but also a particular need and ability. For example, nature (based upon the dialectics of sex) points out the 'need' actually to create life as well as the power to do it. Labour (based upon the dialectics of nature) illustrates the need to produce as well as the power to do it.

Both the dialectics of sex and the dialectics of nature are based upon power, but as we will see the power forms, although related, appear differently:

SEX		NATURE
based on 'nature' power	*vs*	based on 'labour' power
(REPRODUCTION)		(PRODUCTION)

Each dialectic sets up divisions within itself while being in conflict with the other. We may establish these divisions as either the 'natural' division of 'nature' or the 'natural' division of labour:

SEX (species-producing power of reproduction)	NATURE (species power of production)
1 In reality, both men and women have no more no less reproductive power on their own (power to make babies)	1 All humans are as productive of life – both of one's own labour and of fresh life in creation (reproduction and production)
2 Both men and women are necessary for reproduction of life	2 All humans are necessary for production of life
YET	YET
WE HAVE CREATED 'NATURAL' SEX	'NATURAL' DIVISIONS OF LABOUR

		Women *vs* Men		Women's labour *vs* Men's labour	
those who appear more reproductive	those who appear less reproductive			Reproductive ability	Productive ability
NATURAL DIVISION OF 'NATURE'				*NATURAL DIVISION OF LABOUR*	

Also, each dialectic sets up another division which is determined socially or, simply, by society. Thus, we have the social division of the sexes (male, female) and the social division of labour (productive, non-productive):

SEX	*vs*	NATURE
SOCIAL DIVISION OF 'NATURE'		SOCIAL DIVISION OF LABOUR
Both men and women have the ability to be either male, female, passive, dominant, submissive, aggressive.		All humans have the ability to labour and to be equally productive
YET		YET
Society believes through its system of sex relations that not only should men be dominant and aggressive and women female, passive and submissive		Society believes through its system of class relations that many should be productive for the few who are dominant
BUT ALSO		BUT ALSO
that it is natural for sexuality to expose itself and be this way in society.		that it is natural that society be this way

On the one hand, the natural and social divisions of 'nature' within the dialectics of sex create a 'sexual division of nature'. Simply, ideas are formed like 'Men and women are essentially different'; 'Heterosexuality is normal and basically, natural', and 'Sexuality is private' (i.e. our natural instincts should be hidden from others and from society).

On the other hand, the natural and social divisions of labour within the dialectics of nature create the 'sexual division of labour', of which we already have some knowledge. Ideas like 'The family is the "natural" unit of society'; 'A woman's place is in the home'; and 'Monogamy is a "natural form of human behaviour" ' are put forward.

While the dialectics of sex appears to present the idea that 'sex is an instinct, a part of the flow of nature', 'it' successfully thwarts this 'flow' between the sexes. While exposing labour as the reproduction and production of human life, the dialectics of nature separates non-labourer from labourer, reproduction from production and women from men. If we represent the above discussion by a diagram, it appears as follows:

DIALECTICS OF POWER=
(dominant *vs* passive)   (species-producing *vs* species power)
NATURE   *vs* LABOUR
vs   *vs*
SEX   SOCIAL
(male *vs* female)   (non-productive *vs* productive
                          reproduction *vs* production)

OR

DIALECTICS OF POWER = Conflict between SEX AND
                     NATURE, SURVIVAL AND
                     MEANS TO SURVIVE,
                     NATURAL UTILITY AND
                     SOCIAL UTILITY OR
                     REPRODUCTION AND
                     PRODUCTION

DIALECTICS OF POWER =
DIALECTICS OF SEX *vs* DIALECTICS OF NATURE
Major   (dominant *vs* passive)   (species-producing *vs* species
oppositions (male *vs* female)   power)
                                        (life activity *vs* 'conscious '
                                        life activity)

		(reproduction *vs* production)
Based upon 'NATURE' conflict within		LABOUR
Represents 'Needs' HUMAN		'Power'
Creates	Means of reproduction	Means of production
Sets up divisions in 'nature'	*'Natural' division of nature* Although species-producing power is equal between men and women, WOMEN *VS* MEN or women appear to have more species-producing power, while men appear to have less species-produc- ing power. Yet because of this division, MEN *VS* WOMEN or men appear to be physically stronger than women ('naturally' dominant)	*'Natural' division of labour* Although the production of one's own labour and fresh life is equally important for society's survival, REPRO- DUCTION *VS* PRODUC- TION, NON-PRODUCTIVE *VS* PRODUCTIVE
Sets up divisions in 'society'	*Social division of nature* female *vs* male passive *vs* dominant submissive *vs* aggressive	*Social division of labour* productive labour *vs* non- productive labour men's work *vs* women's work male labour *vs* female labour productive labour *vs* domestic labour
	The natural division of nature + the social division of nature = *the sexual division of nature* The sexual division of nature	The natural division of labour + the social division of labour = *the sexual division of labour* The sexual division of labour =

+

THE SEXUAL DIVISION OF POWER

The 'nature' of 'dual organizations': patriarchy vs capitalism

You may rightly question the simultaneous occurrence of two types of organization of power in society. In order to clarify this question, we should look to the field of anthropology and specifically to the work[7] of Lévi-Strauss.

Lévi-Strauss proposes and demonstrates the existence of 'dual organizations'. Dual organizations represent the 'structural similarities' between social systems or a system which is twofold:

> These forms [dual organizations] as described, do not necessarily relate to two different organizations. They may also correspond to two different ways of describing one organization too complex to be formalized by means of a single model.[8]

From this we sense that dual organizations may imply the presence of two reciprocal yet divided facts of human life. In our case, we may view society in terms of patriarchy and capitalism.

We see that within society each system is itself twofold or dialectical – the dialectics of sex and the dialectics of nature, respectively. The crucial point Lévi-Strauss brings out is that it is possible for each of the two elements to be not only reciprocal and opposing but also hierarchically related. In this context, we have established the fact that patriarchy and capitalism are as necessary and equally important in the struggle to alter power and our conception of it. Yet thus far in human history the struggle against capitalism has taken priority over the struggle against patriarchy. A good example of this is the almost total emphasis that has been given to the sexual division of labour in the contemporary feminist movement. In other words, the dialectics of nature takes priority over the dialectics of sex. In the end, divisions between man and women as well as worker and non-worker are never fully understood and thus never challenged totally.

On the level of struggle, our model would resemble the following:

	SEX (PATRIARCHY)	NATURE (CAPITALISM)	
POTEN-	to be pro-sex relations	to be pro-class relations	POTEN-
TIAL FOR	(oppression of 'nature')	(oppression of labour)	TIAL
ANY MAN	anti-feminist	anti-working class	FOR
OR	OR	OR	ANY
WOMEN	to be anti-sex relations	to be anti-class relations	HUMAN

feminist   pro-working class
POWER
(if one is anti-both, one is against
power)
against sexual inequality
against a static concept of 'nature'
and nature itself
against oppressive labour
against misuse of power and
power itself

Ultimately, those who not only feel oppressed but also experience a struggle against power reveal one form of powerlessness. They may try to come to grips with how power affects them most poignantly. They put into practice what they feel. They try to be consistent. That is, they 'as subjects' object to society's treatment of them 'as mere objects', as less than human. They remain powerless, vulnerable and therefore, oppressed in the face of social power.

Historically all oppressed people appear not only to struggle against power but for power in some way. I would contend that the 'nature' of power creates its misuse. In other words, one must not fight 'fire with fire' or power with power. To eliminate power and oppression in society implies the creation of its opposite – powerlessness or possibly, vulnerability.[9]

I have heard people gasp in horror at the above implication. Some have said, 'It's outrageous, mad!' Others say, 'Society cannot exist without power.' True, thus far, society has not existed without power – the misuse of force, creative human force. Imagine. Society has consistently been inconsistent or full of contradictory forces. What would it be like if society was to be consistently consistent? Would struggle, conflict, oppression, even the 'dialectic' disappear? Possibly we would create or re-create a 'truly primitive society – harmonious at one with itself'.[10] Is peace that boring? Is the creative use of human force always contradictory?

One final note

'Naturally' an accolade is bestowed upon any one of you as a reader who after completing this text will not point an accusing finger at lesbians. Rather, the ideal accusation should be directed towards society. As a result, one would incorporate this vision of the level of one's own human experience and struggle.

As we have seen, the lesbian phenomenon presents a challenge to women's position in society. It also challenges the structure of society itself – all power relations. In the light of previous discussions in this chapter, the lesbian struggle against power is represented in the following way:

DIALECTICS OF SEX
Natural division of nature
Society believes that lesbians are 'pseudo-men', not women, but, lesbians are women, structural females.

Social division of nature
Society believes that lesbians are 'social males'. Yet lesbians are women. They should be female. Lesbians appear more male than female. In reality, they are more female-orientated than male-orientated.

DIALECTICS OF NATURE
Natural division of labour
In relationship to men, lesbians are more reproductive. But, lesbians appear as less reproductive than women.

Social division of labour
Lesbians are less productive than men and more productive than women.
As females, they do male work. As 'social males', they are not as productive as males.

POWER STRUGGLE OF LESBIANS
1 Lesbians' struggle against the dialectics of sex;
  (a) they reject the concept of 'nature';
  (b) they reject the differences between men and women or that men are 'naturally' dominant, while women are 'naturally' passive;
  (c) they reject the notions of female and male.
2 Lesbians' struggle against the dialectics of nature;
  (a) they reject that it is natural for a woman to be more sexual because she has a baby and appears more reproductive;
  (b) they reject heterosexuality, the family, monogamy as natural;
  (c) they reject oppressive labour, that is that women's work is less important than men's work.

From all of the above, we see that lesbians expose the roots of power in society. Lesbianism, at a conscious level, has the potential to disrupt the social organization of power. No longer can one say 'Lesbianism is an individual or personal "thing".' Or 'Lesbians are sick people.' Rather, one could say 'Lesbianism is a struggle against all forms of oppression in society.' It is no longer located in an individual woman, but viewed in relationship to the position of all women in society.

Appendix 1
Sample interview

Lesbian Interview Questions

First Name: _____   Date: _____

Occupation: _____   Time: _____

Age: _____   How long: _____

General

1   How would you define lesbianism?

2   Do you see lesbianism as a total way of life? If yes, how is lesbianism a total way of life or in what ways?

3   Do you see lesbianism as a valid or viable way of life for some women in society? If yes, in what ways?

4   How do you think society views the lesbian way of life for some women?

5   How is the lesbian way of life or lesbian experience different from other ways of living open to women?

Lesbian identity

6   Do you see the lesbian identity as a counter-identity for women? In other words, does the lesbian identity exist in society as an identity contrary to what society expects of all women? (i.e., assumption of heterosexuality, wife, mother . . .).
What about woman's identity in itself, can that be viewed as a counter-identity?

7   At what age did you have your first lesbian experience?

8   At what age did you first define yourself as a lesbian?

175

9   Was your first lesbian experience an independent experience, that is, independent of any group identity or group membership? If not, was your first lesbian experience one which came from your involvement in the gay movement or women's movement?

10   Has your definition of lesbianism changed over time? If so, in what ways?

11   What about your ideas about yourself as a lesbian, have they changed over time? Could you say that you see yourself as gradually developing a type of self-awareness that is particular to a lesbian?

12   Do you see your lesbian identity as being a part of or closely linked up with your identity as a woman in society? Another way of asking the question is, can one be both a lesbian and a woman, or do you see them as contradicting one another?

13   Where do you associate with lesbians? How often?

14   Do most people that you associate with know you to be a lesbian?
Work?   School?   What about your family?   How do they react to you?

Lesbianism and feminism

15   Do you see your life as a lesbian as a type of feminism? In what ways?

16   Should lesbianism be a key issue in the women's movement?
In what ways?

in the gay movement?
In what ways?

17   What are your attitudes towards bisexual women?

gay men?

straight men?

18   If you had to place yourself into a category or type of group, how would you define yourself?

lesbian separatist

radical feminist lesbian

women's movement lesbian (came out in women's movement)

gay movement lesbian (came out in gay movement)

non-political lesbian

Appendix 2
Sample letter sent with questionnaire

2 Eldon Grove
London, S.W.3.

Dear Sister,

This is a voluntary questionnaire which I hope you will complete and return to me. At this point in time I am completing a Ph.D. entitled, 'The Sociology of Lesbianism' at the LSE. I am sending out this short questionnaire which will provide a general idea of attitudes, social or political activities, as well as particular lesbian experiences which may be common to all of us. I have started a series of interviews in the London area and want to interview at least 50 interviewees. If you are interested in being interviewed, please write to me at my London address or leave your name and address somewhere on the questionnaire and I'll write to you. Remember, all information is totally confidential and anonymity is a strict rule. Thanks for your help.

Sincerely,

Betsy Ettorre

Appendix 3
Sample questionnaire

Lesbian questionnaire

1   Age   1 _____

2   Occupation   2 _____

3   Religion (if applies)   3 _____

4   How would you define lesbianism? (Check appropriate description – only one)

      (a)   a total way of life or commitment   _____

      (b)   a sexual preference   _____

      (c)   an alternative way of life for women _____

      (d)   a 'deviant' or counter-identity
           in a dominant heterosexual world   _____

5   The lesbian lifestyle could be a valid or viable way of life for (Check one)

      (a)   all women   _____   (d)   few women _____

      (b)   most women _____   (e)   none   _____

      (c)   some women _____

6   Have your ideas about lesbianism or your definition of a lesbian changed over time?

           No _____   Yes   _____

7   If yes, why do you think this has happened?
   Through: (Check one or more)

      (a)   personal experience   _____

      (b)   the women's movement   _____

      (c)   group therapy   _____

      (d)   the gay movement   _____

      (e)   individual therapy   _____

      (f)   other   _____

8 Lesbianism and feminism: (Check one)

    (a)   are totally contradictory   _____
    (b)   do not relate to one another   _____
    (c)   are inseparable   _____
    (d)   somewhat related   _____

9 Do you see your lesbian identity as being very much a part of your identity as a woman in society?

        No _____   Yes _____

10 How often do you associate with other lesbians? (Check one)

    (a)   all of the time   _____
    (b)   most of the time   _____
    (c)   some of the time   _____
    (d)   hardly at all   _____

11 Do you go to: (Check one or more)

    (a)   lesbian bars   _____
    (b)   lesbian political meetings   _____
    (c)   lesbian clubs   _____
    (d)   mixed gay bars (gay men
          and women)   _____
    (e)   mixed gay clubs   _____
    (f)   demonstrations concerning
          women   _____
    (g)   demonstrations concerning
          gays   _____

12 Should lesbianism be a key issue in the women's movement?

        No _____   Yes _____

13 Should lesbianism be a key issue in the gay movement?

        No _____   Yes _____

14 Of the people with whom you associate, how many would you say know you to be a lesbian?

Very few _____ Some _____ Most _____ None _____

What about at work or school?

Very few _____ Some _____ Most _____ None _____

What about your family?

Very few _____ Some _____ Most _____ None _____

15 How do most people react to you when they know you to be a lesbian?

Accepting _____ Indifferent _____ Hostile _____

What about at work or school?

Accepting _____ Indifferent _____ Hostile _____

What about your family reaction?

Accepting _____ Indifferent _____ Hostile _____

16 At what age did you first know yourself to be attracted to women?

17 At what age did you have your first lesbian experience, that is when did you first sleep with a woman? _____

18 At what age did you define yourself as a lesbian? _____

19 Was your first experience:

an independent experience _____

came from involvement in the women's movement _____

from gay movement _____

other (explain) _____

20 (If applies) Has your religion had any effects upon you defining yourself as a lesbian?

Would you say the effects were negative _____ or positive _____ ?

21 Do you read any lesbian, feminist, or gay periodicals?

No _____ Yes _____

22 Do you see the feminist coverage of lesbianism as truly representative of your life as a lesbian?

No _____ Yes _____ In part _____

Do you see the gay coverage of lesbianism as truly representative of your life as a lesbian?

No _____ Yes _____ In part _____

Do you see lesbian coverage of lesbianism as truly representative of your life as a lesbian?

No _____ Yes _____ In part _____

23 Were you ever made to feel 'bad', 'deviant', 'perverse', 'evil', 'ill', 'sinful' . . . by those who know you to be a lesbian?

No _____   Yes _____

By whom? (Check one or more)

(a)   family   _____
(b)   straight friends   _____
(c)   straight sisters in movement   _____
(d)   religious authorities   _____
(e)   legal authorities   _____
(f)   at work   _____
(g)   counsellor or psychiatrist   _____
(h)   other (explain)   _____

24 What are your attitudes towards:

bisexual women   Hostile ___ Indifferent ___ Accepting ___

straight women   Hostile ___ Indifferent ___ Accepting ___

gay men   Hostile ___ Indifferent ___ Accepting ___

straight men   Hostile ___ Indifferent ___ Accepting ___

bisexual men   Hostile ___ Indifferent ___ Accepting ___

25 How do you see yourself? (Check one)

(a)   As a woman who is totally committed to
      women and seeks their company for
      social, emotional, psychological and
      sexual support   _____

(b)   As a woman who is primarily attracted
      to women for emotional, social,
      psychological support but sometimes
      seeks the company of men for the
      satisfaction of these needs   _____

(c)   As a woman who is 'equally' attracted
      to both women and men and seeks
      emotional social, sexual and
      psychological support from both
      men and women 'equally'   _____

(d)   Other (explain)   _____

26 Do you have any children?

No _____ Yes _____ How many? _____

If no, would you like to have a child at some point in the future?

No _____   Yes _____

27   Have you ever been married to a man?

No _____   Yes _____

Have you ever been attracted to a man?

No _____   Yes _____

Have you ever had sex with a man?

No _____   Yes _____

28   If you had to characterize yourself into what category would you place yourself? As a:

(a)   non-political lesbian
(b)   gay movement lesbian (more involved in or came out in this movement)
(c)   women's movement lesbian (more involved in this movement at present or came out in this movement)
(d)   lesbian separatist
(e)   radical feminist lesbian
(f)   'political' lesbian
(g)   other (explain)

Appendix 4
How the data was collected

The data for this study was collected during a period of four years
(1973-7) and was the basis for my Ph.D. research at the University of
London. Four major areas were used for data.

1 Lesbian documents

Books by or about lesbians were used as data as well as gay magazines,
newspapers, journals from Great Britain and the USA. I also found it
useful to examine correspondence which I had with many lesbians over
the course of the four-year period.

2 Field notes

Valuable data was recorded in field notes which represented my
observations of social lesbians in the lesbian ghetto. The field notes
proved useful to me in terms of keeping track of my detailed
observations and were relevant to me in maintaining my research
concerns.

3 Questionnaires

In January 1976 I constructed a questionnaire and distributed it to 700
lesbians. The first set of questionnaires which were distributed
randomly numbered 400. I circulated them at the National Lesbian
Conference which was held in Bristol in February 1976 and which was
attended by approximately 600 women; 101 questionnaires were
returned to me from the Bristol Lesbian Conference. The second set
(300) were distributed randomly to subscribers to *Sappho* magazine in
March 1976. I received 100 questionnaires from the lesbian subscribers.

4 Interviews

Between March 1976 and December 1976 I conducted a series of formal and informal interviews with 60 lesbians. Twenty interviews were taped and formal (I used an interview schedule – see Appendix 1), while the remaining 40 were not taped and I did not follow a set interview schedule. The information from my informal interviews was recorded in my field notes.

Appendix 5
Characteristics of social lesbians who were interviewed

	Age	Occupation	Type	Relationship with men	
				Sexual	Married
1	23	Student Advisor	Sick	No	No
2	20	Student	Sick	No	No
3	24	Lecturer	Sorry	Yes	No
4	50	Writer	Sorry	Yes	Yes
5	29	Computer manager	Sorry	Yes	No
6	26	Manual worker	Sorry	Yes	No
7	28	Musician	Sorry	Yes	Yes
8	28	Journalist	Sorry	Yes	No
9	30	Primary school teacher	Sick	Yes	No
10	22	Publisher's assistant	Sick	Yes	No
11	31	Student	Sorry	Yes	No
12	24	Writer	Sorry	No	No
13	43	Communications director	Sick	Yes	No
14	48	Doctor	Sick	No	No
15	28	Designer	Sorry	Yes	No
16	37	Psychologist	Sorry	Yes	Yes
17	55	Therapist	Sick	Yes	Yes
18	34	Company director	Sick	Yes	Yes
19	29	Retail trade	Sorry	No	No
20	34	Artist	Sorry	Yes	Yes
21	36	Shopkeeper	Sorry	Yes	Yes
22	26	Advertising	Sick	No	No
23	24	Potter	Sorry	Yes	No
24	27	Manual worker	Sorry	Yes	No
25	25	Domestic cleaner	Sorry	Yes	No
26	29	Teacher	Sick	Yes	No
27	28	Teacher	Sorry	Yes	No
28	19	Musician	Sorry	No	No
29	32	Unemployed	Sorry	Yes	Yes
30	23	Factory worker	Sorry	No	No
31	28	Farmer	Sorry	Yes	No
32	25	Civil servant	Sorry	Yes	No
33	24	Primary school teacher	Sorry	Yes	No

	Age	Occupation	Type	Relationship with men	
				Sexual	Married
34	27	Artist	Sick	Yes	No
35	27	Social worker	Sorry	Yes	No
36	25	Civil servant	Sorry	Yes	No
37	35	Lecturer	Sorry	Yes	No
38	25	Administrator	Sorry	Yes	Yes
39	31	Writer	Sick	Yes	Yes
40	32	Mechanic	Sick	Yes	No
41	31	Teacher	Sorry	Yes	No
42	35	Computer programmer	Sorry	Yes	Yes
43	29	Musician	Sorry	Yes	No
44	24	Bookkeeper	Sorry	No	No
45	25	Social worker	Sorry	Yes	No
46	35	Writer	Sick	Yes	No
47	30	Community worker	Sick	No	No
48	22	Domestic worker	Sorry	Yes	No
49	37	Printer	Sorry	Yes	Yes
50	21	Domestic worker	Sick	Yes	No
51	25	Musician	Sorry	Yes	No
52	31	Teacher	Sorry	Yes	No
53	26	Civil servant	Sorry	Yes	No
54	27	Executive secretary	Sick	No	No
55	25	Teacher	Sick	Yes	Yes
56	28	Computer designer	Sorry	Yes	No
57	19	Student	Sick	Yes	No
58	19	Student	Sick	Yes	No
59	29	Shop steward	Sorry	Yes	No
60	35	Unemployed	Sorry	Yes	Yes

Appendix 6

Characteristics of lesbians who were interviewed as compared with lesbians who responded to the questionnaire survey

		INTERVIEWS, N = 60		QUESTIONNAIRES, N = 201		
		No.	%		No.	%
Type	Sick	20	33.3	Sick	100	49.9
	Sorry	40	66.6	Sorry	101	51.1
Relation-	Sexual	11	18.3		61	30.3
ship to		49	81.6		136	67.7
men	Married	12	20.0		48	23.9
		48	80.0		149	74.1

Glossary of terms

Affair	A lesbian relationship which is usually characterized by a short length of time.
Allies	Ideologically orientated lesbians who place more emphasis upon class relations than sex relations.
Bar dyke	A lesbian who frequents lesbian or gay bars.
Bisexual or 'bi'	A woman who appears in a 'marginal area' of lesbian practice and is attracted to both men and women.
Booze-up	A social event which is characterized by drinking.
Bop	To dance.
Born lesbian	A lesbian who feels that she was born a lesbian. (Sick but not sorry types had a tendency to see themselves as 'born' lesbians.)
Busted	To get arrested.
Butch	To be like a man or to be overtly 'male' in dress and character (for some).
Capitalism	One of the dual structures of society which determines the 'nature' of material relations; the mode of production which is historically predominant in society today and which sets up a division of labour between those who own the means of production and those who own nothing but their 'power to produce'.

Celibate	A woman who appears in a 'marginal area' of lesbian practice and who abstains from lesbian sexual activity.
Circle dance	A type of lesbian dance in which a group dances in a circle.
Closet, closeted, closety	To live lesbianism in a 'secretive way'.
Come out	To be open about one's lesbianism.
Consciousness	To be aware of one's historical position as a group in society. Lesbian consciousness develops from apolitical, pre-political and political.
Cruise	To look for a sexual partner.
Crush	To have a general or sexual attraction to another woman.
Custody case	A legal case in which a lesbian mother battles to keep custody of her children, usually after having experienced a divorce from her husband.
Dialectics	A way of looking at society, social change and ourselves as going through the process of transformation. The key to dialectics is that all things in society change through conflict and opposition. Opposites unite or opposing forces become one in the process of change.
Diesel, diesel dyke	A lesbian who is very butch (so butch she can even drive a diesel engine!)
Divorce	To leave a former lover.
Dora	To be thick, stupid (in straight lesbian circles).
Dyke, dykey	To be a lesbian or like one.
Fancy	To be attracted to another.
Feminist	One who is actively concerned with women's oppression.
Femme	To be overtly 'female' (usually in straight lesbian circles).
Fling	To have a fleeting sexual encounter.

Flirt	To make one's sexual attraction obvious to another.
Freak	To have an emotional upheaval.
Gay	Homosexual.
Get it together	To have a sexual encounter.
Ghetto	Area of social activity designated for lesbian social activity.
Ghetto within the ghetto	An area within the general ghetto which tends to be spatially designated.
Goblins	Another name for gay men.
Have a turn	To have a bad emotional experience.
Heavy	To be somewhat oppressive in manner.
Heterosexual, het.	Sexuality which is upheld in society as 'normal' and which exists for men and women.
Ideological lesbianism	The final stage of lesbianism, which is characterized by political consciousness and the linking-up of lesbianism to women's position in society.
Lesbianism	Traditionally it refers to sexual practice (i.e. women who sleep with other women practice lesbianism). However, historically it may also refer to an oppression which some women experience in a society which is patriarchal and capitalist.
Lesbian practice	A complex changing process in which lesbians live out what they feel about themselves.
Lesbian shuffle	A type of lesbian dance.
Non-subservience factor	A finding of this research which reveals that the majority of lesbians in this survey (and, possibly, society) desire not to be subservient to men.
Nora	To be ugly or unattractive in straight lesbian circles.
Marginal areas of lesbian practice	Lesbian practice which appears on the 'fringe' of lesbian social activity or that which is considered as such.

Mixed social setting	Tends to refer to a place or event where men or gay men are present.
Monogamy	To have a primary relationship with one person.
Mother (lesbian)	To appear on the fringe of lesbian practice while, in reality, to be a woman who has children rather than lesbian sex as a priority.
Mrs	Partner in a lesbian relationship.
Multiple relationships	To have a variety of sexual relationships.
Out	To be open about lesbianism.
Patriarchy	One of the dual structures of society which determines the 'nature' of sexual relations; the mode of reproduction which is historically predominant in society today and which sets up a division of the sexes between those who carry babies and those who do not.
Phenomenon	A social occurrence, event or happening which is observable.
Power	The basis of *all* social relationships.
Primary relationship	To have a sexual relationship in which two partners take priority over others in social, or sexual relationships.
Puffs, pufters	Another term for gay men.
Queer	A homosexual.
Rave	To be loud.
Radical feminist (r.f.)	A feminist who sees women's oppression as a result of the biological divisions between men and women.
Real lesbian	A lesbian who feels that she is born a lesbian.
Scene	To have a sexual encounter or areas of 'heightened' lesbian activity.
Secondary relationship	A lesbian lover relationship which is characterized by an involvement that takes a secondary position in the light of one's primary relationship.

Self-chosen lesbian	A lesbian who believes that she has chosen her lesbianism.
Separatists	Ideologically orientated lesbians who place more emphasis upon sex relations than class relations and who choose not to relate to men as a result of this emphasis.
Sexism	The oppressive practice of treating someone (usually a woman in our patriarchal society) as an object of 'sex'.
Sick lesbians	Lesbians in the traditional stage of emergence who believe that they are sick because they are lesbians.
Sick but not sorry lesbians	Social lesbians who tend to be more orientated towards traditional views of themselves than more progressive or ideological views of lesbianism.
Social lesbianism	The historical stage of lesbianism which is characterized by a pre-political consciousness and in which lesbians experience a group identity.
Social males	A term which refers to how society views lesbians, for example, lesbians are women and are aware of being women yet they are viewed as being social males by society.
Society	System of social relationship based upon power.
Sorry but not sick lesbians	Social lesbians who tend to be more orientated towards ideological views of themselves than traditional views of lesbianism.
Split	To leave a lover.
Stars	Lesbians who are well known throughout the ghetto.
Status quo lesbians	Lesbians who do not want to accentuate lesbianism in society, are closeted and do not imitate straight roles. They maintain their 'stakes within the system'.
Straight lesbians	Lesbians who look to the straight world for models of how they should live and be lesbian.

Structural females	A term which refers to the fact that one is capable of carrying a baby before birth. I.e. women are structural females; men are not structural females. Lesbians are structural females because they are women, yet society tends to forget that fact.
Stud	A man.
Traditional lesbianism	The historical stage of lesbianism which emphasizes the individual as well as the sickness syndrome and which appears at a pre-political stage of awareness.
Wank	To waste time, to masturbate.
Wankers	A pejorative term to describe someone.
Wife	A partner.
Women before lesbian factor	A major finding of this study which exposes a high level of women commitment as well as an awareness of being a woman for lesbians.
Women's house	A house which is occupied by all women and which is the basis of emotional support.
Women's liberation movement, WLM	A social movement which develops as a social force in society and which challenges the structure of society *vis à vis* the position of women.

Notes

Introduction — Lesbianism: a personal problem or a women's issue

1 J. Hyatt-Williams, 'Problems of Homosexuality', *British Medical Journal* 3, August 1975, pp. 426-8.

2 In this context, homosexuality refers to both men and women. Yet, traditionally, the word 'homosexual' implied homosexual men more than homosexual women (lesbians).

3 Jeffrey Weeks, *Coming Out: Homosexual Politics in Britain from the Nineteenth Century to the Present*, London, Quartet Books, 1977.

4 A basic assumption of this book is that society is based upon power. In other words, power is the most fundamental process of social life. I would argue that *it is* social life.

5 Throughout this book, lesbians are directly quoted. Unless otherwise indicated, the majority of quotations represent statements from the lives of individual lesbians.

6 Thomas S. Szasz, *The Manufacture of Madness*, St Albans, Paladin, 1973, p. 272.

7 Some argue that to refer to homosexuality as deviant is to collude with society or to uphold its moral values which they feel are dubious. However, if one sees deviance as derived from the master institution of larger society (in our case, patriarchal capitalism), one may also view deviance as actively opposed to society and as originating from the context of the inequality of power, wealth or authority. As we will see, lesbianism is deviant in terms of a male, heterosexual, capitalist society.

8 George Weinberg, *Society and the Healthy Homosexual*, Gerrards Cross, Bucks, Colin Smythe, 1972.

9 Some medical practitioners went so far as to prescribe aversion therapy for their homosexual patients. This treatment involved the use of either drugs or electric shock as punishing stimuli in the presence of homosexual urges in patients. Homosexuals may be targets for new forms of psychiatric treatment.

In 1955 Harold Abramson used Lysergic Acid Diethylamide ꞏ (better known as LSD) on lesbians who were fearful of their homosexual tendencies. He claims that the drug enhanced his

patient's therapeutic development by enabling her to lose her fear
of becoming a lesbian. No comment! See Harold A. Abramson,
'Lysergic Acid Diethylamide (LSD-25) as an Adjunct to
Psychotherapy with Elimination of Fear of Homosexuality',
Journal of Psychology 39, January 1955, pp. 127-55.

10 See especially K. Jay and A. Young, *Out of the Closets: Voices of
Gay Liberation*, New York, Douglas, 1972 for an account of this
trend towards group consciousness.

11 An example of this male bias and non-recognition of lesbians by
gay men is illustrated by G. Hocquenghem (*Homosexual Desire*,
London, Allison and Busby, 1978). Not only does Hocquenghem
have only two references to lesbianism in the subject index but also
he says the following:

> Ours is a phallic society, and the quantity of possible pleasure is
> determined in relationship to the phallus. All sexual acts have an
> aim which gives them their meaning; they are organised into
> preliminary causes which will eventually crystallise in the
> necessary ejaculation, the touchstone of pleasure. It is in this
> sense that the relationship between Chalus and Jupien is
> 'aimless'. The phallus draws on libidinal energy in the same way
> that money draws on labour.
>   Our society is so phallic that the sexual act without
> ejaculation is felt to be a failure. After all, what do men care if
> − as is often the case − the woman remains frigid and feels no
> pleasure? Phallic pleasure is the raison d'être of heterosexuality,
> whichever sex is involved.'

But in this context, I ask what is phallic pleasure for a lesbian if
she neither has a penis nor, furthermore, wants one, as this study
points out. Perhaps the explanation of the 'great signifier' as the
raison d'être of heterosexuality and, implicitly, of homosexuality
is 'limp' because it fails to explain lesbianism, female
homosexuality.

Possibly this is the lesbian threat: theoretically and practically.
A lesbian is a woman who no longer needs phallic explanations.
She no longer remains 'frigid' or under the domain of the phallus.
The lesbian may feel sexual pleasure but the most important and
fundamental pleasure, as we will see, is the freedom or ego-object
choice to be an independent woman. In this way, the lesbian not
only denies the importance of the phallus but actively lives a life
without one penetrating her world.

Hocquenghem's critical study appears to deny the importance
of lesbianism as well as totally subsuming homosexuality under the
domain of the 'sexual'. Because lesbianism is not a sexual
definition, as we will soon discover, Hocquenghem's position is
challenged. Lesbians are not primarily women who sleep with other
women or women who refuse to lie with the phallus. Lesbians are
women who do not represent a lack but affirm a choice as an

oppressed group.

12   Sidney Abbott and Barbara Love, *Sappho was a Right-on Woman: A Liberated View of Lesbianism*, New York, Stein & Day, 1972, p. 20.

13   For example, see David Ward and Gene Kassebaum, 'Homosexuality: A Mode of Adaptation in a Prison for Women', *Social Problems* 12, 2, 1964, pp. 159-77; David Ward and Gene Kassebaum, *Women's Prison: Sex and Social Structure*, London, Weidenfeld & Nicholson, 1965; Rose Giallombardo, 'Social Roles in a Prison for Women', *Social Problems* 13, 3, 1966, pp. 268-89; Rose Giallombardo, *Society of Women: A Study of a Women's Prison*, New York, John Wiley, 1966, and Rose Giallombardo, *The Social World of Imprisoned Girls: A Comparative Study of Institutions for Juvenile Delinquents*, New York, John Wiley, 1974, especially pp. 146-7, 'Lesbianism as a Socializing Agent'.

14   See Charles McCaghy and James K. Skipper, 'Lesbian Behavior as an Adaptation to the Occupation of Stripping', *Social Problems*, 17, 2, 1969, pp. 262-70.

15   J.H. Gagnon and W. Simon express concern for the lesbian as she moves through the various life-cycles which confront *every woman* living in society. However, their analysis is far from being complete. See their classic article, 'Femininity in the Lesbian Community', *Social Problems* 15, 1967, pp. 212-21 and Chapter 6, 'A Conformity Greater than Deviance: The Lesbian' in *Sexual Conduct: The Social Sources of Human Sexuality*, London, Hutchinson, 1973, pp. 176-216.

16   One of the theorists of the 'true believers' is Eli Zaretsky. See Eli Zaretsky, *Capitalism, the Family and the Personal Life*, London, Pluto, 1976.

17   I am grateful to Eva Garmanikov for pointing out this equation to me.

18   For a summary and critique of past explanations within the sociological or general psychological perspectives, see Chapter 2, 'Lesbianism: A Review of Literature' in Elizabeth M. Ettorre, 'The Sociology of Lesbianism: Female "Deviance" and Female Sexuality', unpublished Ph.D. thesis, University of London, 1978.

19   Initially, I planned on taping all 60 interviews. However, I soon realized that the reticence with which my respondents reacted to taping would affect the interview immensely. As a result I decided to tape only 20 interviews and to use another method of recording data from the other 40 interviews. I devised a method whereby after an interview I would go home or into a room by myself and just write — non-stop — what I remembered had been said in the course of the interview. I know that vital information may have been lost in this process. However, in this case, I felt that a situation of informality and a relaxed atmosphere took priority over the collection of explicit detail. Also, I often felt as if I did

recall the major bulk of the interviews, including important data.

Chapter 1 Sappho revisited: a new look at lesbianism

1 Angela Stewart-Park and Jules Cassidy, *We're Here: Conversations with Lesbian Women*, London, Quartet Books, 1977, p. 2.
2 Throughout this chapter, 'material' refers to 'matter of the first class'. In other words, it refers to matter or activity closely related to survival. Sex is usually viewed in this way.
3 The implication here is that sexual behaviour may have 'non-sexual sources', as in the case of a person who masturbates to reduce tension. However, sexual experiences are believed to be constructed from motivations and contexts which are social. See Kenneth Plummer, *Sexual Stigma: An Interactionist Account*, London, Routledge & Kegan Paul, 1975, pp. 32-5, 'The Social Sources of Sexual Meanings'.
4 See Doris and David Jonas, *Sex and Status*, London, Hodder & Stoughton, 1974, especially pp. 144-7 where the authors discuss 'Sex as Competitive Sport'. They contend that sexual performance is rooted in the social context. Traditionally, the privilege of reproducing one's kind was a prize to be competed for. Today the prize, sex itself, has become the arena.
5 Traditionally women's productive function has been minimized. However, recently this point has been challenged and domestic labour is viewed as valuable in economic terms. See Jean Gardiner, 'Political Economy of Domestic Labour in Capitalist Society' in *Dependence and Exploitation in Work and Marriage*, edited by Diana Leonard Barker and Sheila Allen, London, Longman, 1976; also Jean Gardiner, 'Woman, the Labour Process and Class Structure' in *Class and Class Structure*, edited by Alan Hunt, London, Lawrence & Wishart, 1977.
6 Simone de Beauvoir, *The Second Sex*, New York, Bantam Books, 1970, p. 33.
7 Nicole Claude-Mathieu, *Ignored by Some, Denied by Others: The Social Sex Category in Sociology*, London, Women's Research and Resources Centre Publications, 1977, pp. 8-9.
8 Sidney Abbott and Barbara Love, *Sappho was a Right-on Woman: A Liberated View of Lesbianism*, New York, Stein & Day, 1972, p. 47.
9 For an insight into the gay movement and its developing consciousness, see Jeffrey Weeks, *Coming Out: Homosexual Politics in Britain from the Nineteenth Century to the Present*, London, Quartet, 1977; Dennis Altman, *Homosexual: Oppression and Liberation*, London, Allen Lane, 1974 and Karla Jay and Allen Young (eds), *Out of the Closets: Voices of Gay Liberation*, New York, Douglas Books, 1972. For a view of lesbianism as it relates to the women's movement see, Stewart-Park and Cassidy, *op. cit.*

and Abbott and Love, *op cit*.

10   Brake discusses the 'new consciousness' of sexual minority groups and their contemporary emergence. See Mike Brake, 'I May be Queer, But at least I am a Man' in Diana Leonard Barker and Sheila Allen (eds), *Sexual Divisions and Society: Process and Change*, London, Tavistock, 1976.

11   Kate Millett, *Sexual Politics*, New York, Avon Books, 1969.

12   Queen Victoria would not believe that it could ever exist. After the passage of the Criminal Law Amendment Bill in 1885 (making homosexual acts between adults punishable by law), Queen Victoria refused to sign the Bill until all the references to women were deleted. Lesbianism was unthinkable to the Queen!

13   For some biographical insights into the life of one of these women, read Vera Brittain, *Radclyffe Hall: A Case of Obscenity?*, London, Femina Books. 1968.

14   Unless, as Jane Rule suggests, a woman was 'safely married and dressed and behaved like a women – in public anyway', as did Virginia Woolf and Vita Sackville-West. See Jane Rule, *Lesbian Images*, London, Peter Davies, 1975.

15   Radclyffe Hall, *The Well of Loneliness*, London, Jonathan Cape, 1928.

16   This term is used in this context to show the existence of opposing forces.

17   Gardiner (1977), *op. cit*.

18   However, there are ways for lesbians to get pregnant and become mothers. One way is through AID, a method of artificial insemination.

Chapter 2 The social reality of lesbianism

1   Erving Goffman, *Stigma: Notes on the Management of Spoiled Identity*, Harmondsworth, Penguin, 1963.

2   Sidney Abbott and Barbara Love, *Sappho was a Right-on Woman: A Liberated View of Lesbianism*, New York, Stein & Day, 1972, p. 64.

3   Shulamith Firestone, *The Dialectic of Sex*, New York, Bantam Books, 1970, p. 128.

Chapter 3 Social lesbians and social lesbianism: Who are they? What is 'it'?

1   Thomas S. Szasz, *The Manufacture of Madness*, St Albans, Paladin, 1973, p. 192.

2   For an account of the legal ramifications concerned with homosexuality in Britain, see H. Montgomery Hyde, *The Other Love: An Historical and Contemporary Survey of Homosexuality in Britain*, London, Mayflower, 1970 especially pp. 199-205, and

Jeffrey Weeks, *Coming Out: Homosexual Politics in Britain from the Nineteenth Century to the Present*, London, Quartet Books, 1977, especially pp. 169-82.
3 See Herbert Blumer, 'Social Movements' in Barry McLaughlin (ed.), *Studies in Social Movements*, New York, Free Press, 1969, pp. 8-29 for an interesting discussion of this phenomenon.

Chapter 4 'Sick but not sorry' vs 'sorry but not sick': the born lesbian and the self-chosen lesbian

1 As you may recall, the mean age for social lesbians was 30 years of age. It is interesting to note here that the Sappho group's mean age was 34, while the Conference lesbians' mean age was 26. These age differences correspond somewhat to the generational standpoint as well as specific lesbian orientation from which each group emerged and towards which each group ultimately moves.
2 For an interesting discussion of this concept (but with more emphasis upon male homosexuals than lesbians), see 'The Model Psychiatric Scapegoat – the Homosexual' in Thomas S. Szasz, *The Manufacture of Madness*, St Albans, Paladin, 1973, pp. 272-88.
3 Cynthia Fuchs Epstein discusses these expectations in *Woman's Place: Options and Limits in Professional Careers*, Berkeley, University of California Press, 1970.

Chapter 5 Lesbian consciousness and lesbian practice

1 In this chapter, social lesbian practice does not include the practice of those lesbians who tend to be ideologically-orientated. The following chapter will discuss political practice for lesbians. However, we must not forget the progression which some lesbians experience as they develop their consciousness and move towards ideology.
2 S. Abbott and B. Love, *Sappho was a Right-on Woman: A Liberated View of Lesbianism*, New York, Stein & Day, 1972, p. 101.
3 One lesbian described this transition and how she viewed bisexuals:

> 'I don't think women are fucking over other women when they are bisexual. I look on it as a transition period, a sort of stepping stone, but then they might step back. It's sort of a testing ground. They don't quite dare leap . . . . Then I think that they are just as capable of stepping backwards, you know, if the water is too cold, than of stepping across.'

Chapter 6 The emergence of political consciousness: lesbian feminism as an ideological form

1. Roberta Salper, 'The Development of the American Women's Liberation Movement, 1967-1971', in Roberta Salper, (ed.), *Female Liberation: History and Current Politics*, New York, Alfred Knopf, 1972.
2. Lesbian feminism is synonymous with radical lesbianism. For the purposes of this text, I have chosen to use lesbian feminism rather than radical lesbianism. I do not want to confuse the latter term with radical feminism. Although both radical feminism and radical lesbianism imply a feminist critique of society, they effect variety in practice. In other words, different choices are made and these are dependent upon one's particular position in the general WLM.
3. Jo Freeman, 'The Women's Liberation Movement: Its Origins, Structures, Impact and Ideas', in Jo Freeman (ed.), *Women: A Feminist Perspective*, Palo Alto, California, Mayfield Publishing Company, 1975, p. 455.
4. Amos Hawley, 'Community Power and Urban Renewal Success', *American Journal of Sociology* 68, January 1963, pp. 422-31.
5. Marvin Olsen, 'Power as a Social Process' in Marvin Olsen, (ed.), *Power in Societies*, New York, Macmillan, 1970, pp. 2-10.
6. M.L. Carden, *The New Feminist Movement*, New York, Russell Sage Foundation, 1974, p. 53.
7. For an interesting discussion of the GLF, see Jeffrey Weeks, *Coming Out: Homosexual Politics in Britain from the Nineteenth Century to the Present*, London, Quartet Books, 1977, especially Chapter 16, 'The Gay Liberation Front, 1970-72', pp. 185-206.
8. This information was related to me by a former GLF lesbian.
9. This notion of society itself as embodying a contradiction will be discussed in the final chapter. There, we will see how the 'dual' structure of society creates human tensions.
10. I am grateful to Eva Garmanikov for her insights in this area but, most of all, for sharing them with me.
11. See E.M. Ettorre, 'The Sociology of Lesbianism: Female "Deviance" and Female Sexuality', unpublished Ph.D. Thesis, University of London, 1978.
12. Pre-feminist refers to one who has a consciousness of 'women's politics' in a vague sense, but who has not transformed this consciousness into political activity or active struggle with others who have a feminist consciousness.
13. It is interesting to note that the lesbian ally tendency was in seed form during the initial stages of the lesbian feminist ghetto. However, some of the founding members of the lesbian feminist ghetto had already been allied to some group prior to the ghetto's existence. However, they were somewhat discouraged with their alliance and subsequently left. Therefore, this tendency was often suppressed during the development of the lesbian feminist ghetto.

14 Tony Jefferson, in his discussion of 'Teds', points out that they
    have a strong sense of themselves as a group. This group-mindedness
    created a desire 'to hold on to territory which was being
    expropriated from them.' Fights in defence of 'their space'
    resulted. This process reflects somewhat the tensions which they
    experienced when they perceived the lesbian feminists as a threat
    to their 'territorial space' (the newly acquired pub). See Tony
    Jefferson, 'Cultural Responses of the Ted' in Stuart Hall and Tony
    Jefferson (eds), *Resistance through Rituals: Youth Subcultures in
    Post-war Britain*, London, Hutchinson, 1975, pp. 81-6.

Afterword — The lesbian struggle: sex vs class or nature vs labour?

1   Marx discusses the notion of the dialectics within nature in *The
    Economic and Philosophic Manuscripts of 1844*. He says, 'Man is
    directly a natural being . . . a human natural being.' In other words,
    'Man' is endowed with life, or what Marx calls, 'active natural
    being', 'natural powers' or 'vital powers'. Human life or these
    'powers' causes 'man' to suffer because one must go outside of
    oneself in order to satisfy one's need. In other words, there is a
    tension between one's needs and the power to fulfill them as well
    as between one's instincts and the objects of one's instincts. (For
    Marx, labour, eating and sex would be included among human
    instincts).
         Therefore, Marx maintains that 'man' only 'creates or posits
    these objects because he is posited by objects — because at bottom
    he is nature'. Although Marx claims to reject human nature, he also
    appears to accept 'it'. History is the continual transformation of
    human nature, for Marx. However, I would argue that he limits the
    possibility for this transformation. In other words, what is primary
    for Marx is that 'the objects of man's instincts exist outside
    himself' and that 'as a natural, corporeal, sensuous, objective being
    he is suffering, conditioned and limited creature, like animals and
    plants'. In other words, 'man' struggles because he has certain
    needs which are fulfilled. Needs and the power to fulfill these
    needs create suffering. Or, NEEDS+POWER=STRUGGLE.
         Yet, I would argue that what is important is not so much the
    fulfillment of our needs by 'objects' outside ourselves i.e. I have
    hunger; I have to get food. Rather, what is primary and
    furthermore, very crucial is that *struggle occurs prior to obtaining
    the object of one's needs*. In other words, *struggle for* rather than
    the power to do something is more important. This is a factor
    which Marx was unaware of. NEEDS+STRUGGLE=POWER. It is
    the dialectics of power, human power.
         Within this view, the power to fulfill the object of one's needs is
    the result of struggle for a specific 'need' rather than the object of
    the need itself. Therefore, struggle becomes the link between the

subject (needs) and the object (power) and not the result of the links between the subject and the object. We are therefore left with a total questioning of the existence of human nature as well as the notion of instinct (other than eating). 'Nature power' (dialectic of sex) not labour power (dialectic of nature) is our starting point.

For an interesting discussion of the above ideas, see K. Marx, *Economic and Philosophic Manuscripts of 1844*, Moscow, Progress Publishers, 1959.

2   For a discussion of this position, see Shulamith Firestone, *The Dialectic of Sex, The Case for the Feminist Revolution*, New York, Bantam Books, 1970.

3   Compromise in this context is used in the traditional way. It implies some sort of mutual settlement in which one group may change more than the other.

4   Man 'objectifies' his 'nature'; therefore, he masters 'it'. He changes the world around himself. For Marx, labour brings about this essential distinction of man. Cf. Frederick Engels, *Dialectics of Nature*, Moscow, Progress Publishers, 1934, especially pp. 176-80.

5   The laws of dialectics or development of history of nature and human society can be reduced to: the law of the transformation of quantity into quality and vice versa; the law of the interpenetration of opposites; the law of the negation of the negation (see *ibid.*, p. 62).

6   Dialectic = 'Human Nature'.

7   C.f. Claude Lévi-Strauss, *Structural Anthropology*, Harmondsworth, Penguin, 1963, especially Chapter VIII, 'Do Dual Organizations Exist?', pp. 132-63.

8   *Ibid.*, p. 134.

9   See Firestone, *op. cit.*, especially Chapter 6, *'Love'*, pp. 126-45. Firestone argues that vulnerability (which in reality is 'true love') must be an exchange of selves totally. This obviously breaks down all forms of power between people.

10   Lévi-Strauss, *op. cit.*, p. 117.

Bibliography

Abbott, S. and Love, B. (1972), *Sappho was a Right-on Woman: A Liberated View of Lesbianism*, New York, Stein & Day.

Abramson, H.A. (1955), 'Lysergic Acid Diethylamide (LSD-25) III as an Adjunct to Psychotheraphy with Elimination of Fear of Homosexuality' in *Journal of Psychology* 39, pp. 127-55.

Altman, D. (1974), *Homosexual: Oppression and Liberation*, London, Allen Lane.

Atkinson, T. (1974), *Amazon Odyssey*, New York, Links.

Barker, D.L. and Allen, S. (eds), (1976), *Sexual Divisions and Society: Process and Change*, London, Tavistock Press.

Barker, D.L. and Allen, S. (eds) (1976), *Dependence and Exploitation in Work and Marriage*, London, Longman.

Blumer, H. (1969), 'Social Movements' in B. McLaughlin (ed), *Studies in Social Movements*, New York, Free Press.

Boston Women's Health Collective (1973), *Our Bodies Ourselves*, New York, Simon & Schuster.

Brake, M. (1976), 'I May be Queer but at least I am a Man' in D. Barker and S. Allen (eds), *Sexual Divisions and Society: Process and Change*, London, Tavistock Press.

Brittain, V. (1968), *Radclyffe Hall: A Case of Obscenity?*, London, Femina Books.

Brown, R.M. (1973), *Rubyfruit Jungle*, Plainfield, Vermont, Daughters Inc.

Carden, M.L. (1974), *The New Feminist Movement*, New York, Russell Sage Foundation.

Chapman, D. (1965), 'What is a Lesbian?' in *Man and Society 9*, pp. 34-8.

Chesler, P. (1972), *Women and Madness*, New York, Avon Books.

Claude-Mathieu, N. (1977), *Ignored by Some, Denied by Others: the Social Sex Category in Sociology*, London, WRRC Publications.

Daniel, S. (1954), 'The Homosexual Woman in Present Day Society' in *International Journal of Sexology*, 7, 4, pp. 223-4.

De Beauvoir, S. (1970), *The Second Sex*, New York, Bantam Books.

Engels, F. (1934), *Dialectics of Nature*, Moscow, Progress Publishers.

Epstein, C.F. (1970), *Woman's Place: Options and Limits in Professional Careers*, Berkeley, University of California Press.

Ettorre, E.M. (1978), *The Sociology of Lesbianism: Female "Deviance" and Female Sexuality*, unpublished Ph.D. thesis, University of London.

Firestone, S. (1970), *The Dialectic of Sex: the Case for Feminist Revolution*, New York, Bantam Books.

Freeman, J. (1975), 'The Women's Liberation Movement: Its Origins, Structures, Impact and Ideas' in J. Freeman (ed.), *Women: A Feminist Perspective*, Palo Alto, California, Mayfield Publishing Co.

Furlong, M. (1966), 'Paradoxes of Love', *Man and Society* 10, pp. 39-40.

Gagnon, J.H. and Simon, W. (1967), 'Femininity in the Lesbian Community', *Social Problems* 15, pp. 212-21.

Gagnon, J.H. and Simon, W. (1973), *Sexual Conduct: The Social Sources of Human Sexuality*, London, Hutchinson.

Gardiner, J. (1976), 'Political Economy of Domestic Labour in Capitalist Society' in D.L. Barker and S. Allen (eds), *Dependence and Exploitation in Work and Marriage*, London, Longman.

Gardiner, J. (1977), 'Woman, the Labour Process and Class Structure' in A. Hunt (ed.), *Class and Class Structure*, London, Lawrence & Wishart.

Gebhard, P.H., Raboch, J. and Giese, H. (1970), *The Sexuality of Women*, London, Andre Deutsch.

Giallombardo, R. (1966), 'Social Roles in a Prison for Women', *Social Problems* 13, 3, pp. 268-89.

Giallombardo, R. (1966), *Society of Women: A Study of A Women's Prison*, New York, John Wiley.

Giallombardo, R. (1974), *The Social World of Imprisoned Girls*, New York, John Wiley.

Goffman, E. (1963), *Stigma: Notes on the Management of Spoiled Identity*, Harmondsworth, Penguin.

Hall, R. (1928), *The Well of Loneliness*, London, Jonathan Cape.

Hawley, A. (1963), 'Community Power and Urban Renewal Success', *American Journal of Sociology* 68, pp. 422-3.

Hopkins, J. (1969), 'The Lesbian Personality', *British Journal of Psychiatry* 155, pp. 1433-6.

Hyatt-Williams, J. (1975), 'Problems of Homosexuality', *British Medical Journal* 3, 426-8.

Hyde, H.M. (1970), *The Other Love*, London, Mayflower.

Jay, K. and Young, A. (1972), *Out of the Closets: Voices of Gay Liberation*, New York, Douglas.

Jefferson, T. (1975), 'Cultural Responses of the Ted' in T. Jefferson and S. Hall (eds), *Resistance through Rituals*, London, Hutchinson.

Johnston, J. (1970), *Lesbian Nation: A Feminist Solution*, New York, Simon & Schuster.

Jonas, D. and D. (1974), *Sex and Status*, London, Hodder & Stoughton.

Kinsey, A.C., Wardell, B., Pomeroy, C.E. and Gebhard, P.H. (1953), *Sexual Behaviour in the Human Female*, Philadelphia, W.B. Saunders.

Klaich, D. (1975), *Woman Plus Woman: Attitudes toward Lesbianism*, London, New English Library.

Lévi-Strauss, C. (1963), *Structural Anthropology*, Harmondsworth, Penguin.

McCaghy, C. and Skipper, J.K. (1969), 'Lesbian Behavior as an Adaptation to the Occupation of Stripping', *Social Problems* 17, 2, pp. 262-70.

McIntosh, M. (1968), 'The Homosexual Role', *Social Problems* 16, pp. 182-92.

Magee, B. (1965), 'The Facts about Lesbianism: A Special Inquiry into a Neglected Problem', *New Statesman* 69,1176, pp. 491-3.

Martin, D. and Lyon, P. (1972), *Lesbian/Woman*, New York, Bantam Books.

Marx, K. (1959), *Economic and Philosophic Manuscripts of 1844*, Moscow, Progress Publishers.

Morgan, R. (1970), *Sisterhood is Powerful*, New York, Random House.

Mozes, E. (1951), 'The Lesbian . . .', *Sexology* 19, 5, pp. 294-9.

Olsen, M. (1970), 'Power as a Social Process' in M. Olsen (ed.), *Power in Societies*, New York, Macmillan.

Plummer, K. (1975), *Sexual Stigma: An Interactionist Account*, London, Routledge & Kegan Paul.

Rosen, D. (1974), *Lesbianism: A Study of Female Homosexuality*, Springfield, Illinois, Charles C. Thomas.

Rule, J. (1975), *Lesbian Images*, London, Peter Davies.

Salper, R. (1972), 'The Development of the American Women's Liberation Movement, 1967-1971', in R. Salper (ed.), *Female Liberation: History and Current Politics*, New York, Knopf.

Stearn, J. (1965), *The Grapevine: A Report on the Secret World of the Lesbian*, London, Frederick Muller.

Stevenson, M.L. (1968), 'Living with a Stigma: A Study of 11 Female Homosexual Couples', urpublished M.A. thesis, University of Essex.

Stewart-Park, A. and Cassidy, J. (1977), *We're Here: Conversations with Lesbian Women*, London, Quartet Books.

Szasz, T. (1973), *The Manufacture of Madness*, St Albans, Paladin.

Taylor, A.J.W. (1965), 'The Significance of "Darls" or "Special Relationships" for Borstal Girls', *British Journal of Criminology* 5, 4, pp. 406-18.

Ward, D. and Kassebaum, G. (1964), 'Homosexuality: A Mode of Adaptation in a Prison for Women', *Social Problems* 12, 2, pp. 159-77.

Ward, D. and Kassebaum, G. (1965), *Women's Prison: Sex and Social Structure*, London, Weidenfeld & Nicholson.

Ward, D. and Kassebaum, G. (1970) 'Lesbian Liaison' in J.H. Gagnon and W. Simon (eds), *The Sexual Scene*, Chicago, Aldine.

Weeks, J. (1977), *Coming Out: Homosexual Politics in Britain from the Nineteenth Century to the Present*, London, Quartet Books.

Weinberg, G. (1972), *Society and the Healthy Homosexual*, Gerrards Cross, Colin Smythe.

Wolff, C. (1977), *Love Between Women*, London, Duckworth.
Zaretsky, E. (1976), *Capitalism, the Family and the Personal Life*,
    London, Pluto Press.

Note   The references which are cited in the bibliography include not
only those which are in the text but also those which may be of interest
to the reader. I have included articles and books which reflect a 'lesbian
theme'. Readers will also note that I have eliminated major
psychoanalytic, psychiatric and psychological sources. My initial desire
was to include them. However, after thinking about their inclusion in
the bibliography, I decided that I would eliminate most of the works
which perpetuated the idea that lesbianism was an abnormality, a
psychological sickness, a disease, etc. Thus, I would not continue to
perpetuate these misconceptions.

Index

Lesbian feminist ghetto, 151-5
Lesbian ghetto, 50-6
Lesbian identity, 75, 77-8; *see also*
  Counter-identity
Lesbianism, 190; and feminism, 8,
  77-81, 125-9, 145-56; and power,
  9, 122, 125, 173; and sociology, 8;
  three forms of, 70-3, 118, 160,
  190, 192-3
Lesbian mothers, 137-8, 191
Lesbian relationships, 48-69
Lesbians and the police, 52, 155
Lesbian separatists, 14, 68-9, 111, 149-
  149-51, 160, 192

Marginal areas, 134-8, 190
Marxist dialectic, 163
Marxist feminism, 145, 161-2
Monogamy, 56-7, 60, 169, 191
Motherhood, 3, 31, 121; *see also*
  Lesbian mothers
Multiple relationships, 56, 58-60, 191

Non-subservience factor, 85-8, 190

Occupations, *see* Social lesbians

Patriarchy, 8-9, 88, 145, 151, 159-61,
  191
Patriarchy/Capitalism, as a dual
  structure, 9, 17, 161, 171
Political lesbianism, 145-6
Pre-feminism, 153
Primary relationships, 56, 60-1, 191
Prisons, 8
Pub war, 155

Radical feminism, 145, 161
Real lesbian, 145, 161, 191
Religion, *see* Social lesbians
Revolutionary feminism, 145

Sappho: lesbian journal, 51, 97,
  183; London group 11, 96-8;
  poetess, 24, 70
Saturnalia, 70
Secondary relationships, 56, 61, 191
Self-chosen lesbian, 99-100, 132, 192
Separatism, *see* Lesbian separatists
Sexual division of labour, 2-3, 8-9,
  19-20, 30-1, 144, 159, 161-2, 171
Sexual division of power, 161-70

Sexuality, and power, 17
Sexual Offences Act (1967), 71
'Sick but not sorry', *see* Social lesbians,
  two types of
Sixth Demand, 147-8
Social females, 20
Social lesbianism, 192; implications of,
  75-95; related to other forms, 158,
  160
Social lesbians: and change, 92-3,
  100-3; comparison of two types,
  96-117, 119-20, consciousness of,
  89, 123; and lesbian practice,
  131-8; occupations of, 114-15;
  relations with men, 85-8; and
  religion, 116-17; society's reaction
  to, 93-4, 112; two types of, 26-30,
  192; and women's position, 77-85;
  see also Counter-identity, Gay
  movement, Women's movement
Social males, 20, 31-2, 192; related
  to lesbian struggle, 171; related to
  social lesbians, 81
Social tolerance, 119-20
Social view, *see* Lesbianism, forms of,
  Social lesbianism
Society, a system of power, 17, 143-4,
  157, 192
'Sorry, but not sick', *see* Social
  lesbians, two types of
Squatting, 153
Status quo lesbians, 132-3, 192
Straight lesbians, 62, 131-2, 192
Stripping, 8
Structural females, 31-2, 81, 88, 173,
  193
Szasz, T., 5, 71

Traditional view, *see* Lesbianism,
  forms of
Transsexuals, 151

Victoria, Queen, 71

Women before lesbian factor, 77, 193
Women's Liberation Movement
  (WLM), 73, 193; ideological splits,
  149-56; and lesbian politics, 146-8;
  related to social lesbians, 79-80;
  theory and practice, 63, 142-3
Women's movement, and social
  lesbians, 79-80

For Product Safety Concerns and Information please contact our EU
representative GPSR@taylorandfrancis.com
Taylor & Francis Verlag GmbH, Kaufingerstraße 24, 80331 München, Germany